# When It All Falls Apart

## A Story of Hope and Healing

### Robert B. Haase

Burton Press International
Attention: Permissions Coordinator
1910 4th Ave E Unit 234
Olympia, WA 98506

ISBN 978-1-7351710-5-0 (Paperback)
ISBN 978-1-7351710-6-7 (Hard Cover)
ISBN 978-1-7351710-7-4 (Audio Book)
ISBN 978-1-7351710-4-3 (Kindle eBook)

**BPI**

Cover design by Burton Press International.

Published by Burton Press International

www.notwhatyouhadplanned.org

**The meaning behind the cracked bowl image on the cover:**

Kintsugi (金継ぎ), meaning "golden joinery," is a Japanese art of repairing broken pottery using lacquer mixed with powdered precious metals like gold, silver, or platinum. Originating in the 15th century when shogun Ashikaga Yoshimasa sought a more aesthetic repair for his broken tea bowl, artisans developed this method to transform damage into beauty. Kintsugi embodies the concept of Wabi-Sabi—appreciating imperfection—and symbolizes resilience by turning flaws into unique features. Serving as a metaphor for life's challenges, it inspires finding strength and beauty in imperfections.

# DEDICATION

I dedicate this book to my daughters, Ashley, Sara, and Holly, my sister, Lisa, and my parents, Robert L. and Violet Haase. Your love and sacrifices sustained me through my most challenging times. You stood by me with unwavering compassion, ensuring my safety and comfort when I needed it most.

To my family, friends, and my incredible Facebook community, thank you for your prayers and encouragement during my darkest hours. Your kindness and encouragement meant more than words can express.

I am truly a blessed man.

# FOREWARD

I first met Bob Haase in 2014 when he attended one of the first Cancer Survivor Celebrations that I coordinate as a Psycho-Oncology Consultant for the Providence Regional Cancer System in Olympia Washington. After learning about his cancer experience, I asked him to speak at the event a couple years later. It was clear that it was not his first public speaking gig! His confidence, humor, and optimism softened the intense narrative – the audience was captivated and heartened by his very ability to speak. He described in detail years of symptoms prior to a diagnosis, intense treatment, and the aftermath. A few years later he interviewed me for his first book, Not What You Had Planned: Finding Strength and Hope in the Storms of Adversity. And now several years later I am honored to be writing the foreward for this book, When it All Falls Apart: A Story of Hope and Healing.

I first heard of Bob's recurrence on Facebook. He posted regularly and I was in awe of his ability to share so much in the midst of a terrifying ordeal. I was also devastated that he had to go through it all over again and this time with more trauma and loss. I was not surprised by his openness because all my interactions with Bob have been characterized by what I cherish most about my work with many people diagnosed with cancer and their loved ones: an accelerated authenticity best described as intense and beautiful conversations about the most critical aspects of being alive.

I often describe a cancer diagnosis as an abrupt and unwanted yank out of the proverbial cave that so many of us live in – a den of denial where we do not believe we will ever get sick, let alone die. Whether one is wrenched out by their prostate, breast, or tongue, it is blinding and scary out of that cave. Others may try to keep you in the darkness where there is an illusion of safety. Yet the light makes things very clear; you can see what is important, recognize that life is limited for all, and understand that we often have more choice than we think.

Some may think that they cannot embrace life unless they are "cured" of disease, but my years of working with cancer patients have taught me that this is inaccurate. I have known many people with early-stage disease that never recurs who are not healed. They are not at peace. And conversely, I have known many with stage 4, often incurable disease who are healed. So, healing and curing are not synonymous. This book, as the title promises, is about healing and hope – no matter the stage or prognosis or estimated life expectancy. [I actually never use the word cured, I prefer No Evidence of Disease or NED because it is a more accurate description: as best as can be seen right now, there is no evidence of disease but we cannot guarantee that will always be the case.]

No matter one's diagnosis or prognosis we are alive until we are dead. I once heard that HOPE means Hang On, Possibilities Exist! How do we want to spend our days? Whether considered NED, living with cancer as more of a chronic disease that never goes away but can be managed for a span of time, on hospice, or somewhere in between all these points? Perhaps it is not cancer, but some other intense adversity or challenge that feels insurmountable. Now what? What to focus on, what to say to oneself, and what to say to those who are in the midst of a storm?

Mark Nepo, the poet and cancer survivor, says that what is not expressed is depressed. I kept thinking of those words as I read this book because Bob so poignantly and accurately expresses what at times feels like an unbearable trial. He, along with his loving daughters and parents, lets us in to witness their pain, joy, faith, gratitude, and love. I love hearing the different perspectives of each family member because we know a cancer diagnosis and treatment affect more than just the one diagnosed with the disease. Caregivers and companions often feel that they cannot express their own pain in their desire to protect the patient. And yet, as the flight attendant always reminds us, you must put the oxygen mask over your own mouth first because if you are not breathing you cannot help anyone else.

What a privilege for all readers, no matter the specifics of the adversity faced, to be educated and supported by such wise souls as Bob and his family. There are great lessons to be learned here, taught to us by an extraordinary man who even after losing his voice is speaking to us loud and clear. Please listen . . .


Cobie Whitten PhD

*Cobie has a doctorate in Clinical Psychology from the University of Illinois at Urbana-Champaign and has extensive experience working with cancer patients and their loved ones. She is a Psycho-Oncology Consultant for the Providence Regional Cancer System (since 2008) and a faculty member at Harmony Hill Retreat Center. Previously, Cobie worked for the Washington State Department of Health in the Washington Breast & Cervical Health Program, co-chaired the Survivorship, Palliative Care & End-of-Life Issues Taskforce of Washington CARES About Cancer, was an Expert Speaker for Pfizer, and taught at Saint Martin's University.*

# PART ONE

## MY PERSONAL JOURNEY

# The Journey Unfolds

In 2006, I had just finished preparing dinner for my second wife and youngest daughter, Holly. I remember sitting at the dining room table and sprinkling salt on my potatoes. I took a bite and immediately felt a burning pain on the left underside of my tongue. It was a different kind of pain than burning my tongue on hot food or eating something spicy. I loved spicy food, but this wasn't the same sensation. I shrugged it off and didn't think much about it until the same thing happened the following morning when I put salt on my eggs. "What's the deal?" I thought as I got up and went into the bathroom. With a flashlight in my left hand, I lifted my tongue up with my right hand and could see a thin white line on the otherwise pink tissue.

Over the next week, the pain from salty foods slowly worsened, and I eventually—and begrudgingly —called my family doctor's office and made an appointment to see him in the coming week. In the meanwhile, the pain persisted, which was frustrating. I liked salt in my food.

The appointment time couldn't have come fast enough because the pain had been gradually increasing. My doctor was a general practitioner with some experience seeing other patients with a similar condition, but not much. After lifting my tongue with an oversized tongue depressor, he looked through his magnification goggles, squinted his eyes, and said, "Well, Mr. Haase, I see some superficial white cells. You likely have a condition called leukoplakia, a condition that starts for reasons unknown. The most likely start would come from long-term tobacco use (nope) or long-term high alcohol consumption. He said, "Unless you've been tossing back a fifth of hard alcohol daily for years, I don't know what it could be from, but we should keep an eye on it." *No kidding*, I thought. He sent me home with a topical ointment, which helped the pain, but nothing changed, and the white cells persisted.

Over the next couple of months, the pain slowly worsened, so I called my doctor's office again. I spoke with his nurse, who said, "Let me talk with the doctor, and I'll call you back." She did so an hour later.

"Bob, the doctor wants you to see our in-house otolaryngologist, our ENT." I interrupted her, asking, "Your *what?*" She replied, "He's an Ear, Nose, and Throat specialist. He's the one you want to see." His schedule was full for several months, but he extended his hours to make time to see me nonetheless.

I endured a few more weeks of pain until it was time to sit in the ENT's examination chair. "I need to numb the area on the underside of your tongue and scrape off the cells for the pathologist to inspect," he explained. I saw the three-inch-long needle, and my body stiffened a bit. "Breathe," he said calmly. "Just a small pinch, and you'll be set."

The biopsied tissue was evaluated by the pathologist, testing it for cancer. A few days later, the ENT called and said, "Good news! It's not cancer!" But the pain seemed to dissipate for about six months, only to return like an annoying houseguest. The process would repeat itself every four to six months until the last call in the summer of 2008. When he repeated the familiar phrase, "It's not cancer!" I followed with, "I'm also not pregnant." Over a year of cut-and-test and still the same answer. He could feel my frustration.

I felt bad about letting my frustrations spill out on my ENT. Although he understood, he didn't deserve that. The next time I came in for a scraping of cells, the doctor cut out a larger swath of tissue, which he sent to several labs throughout the US.

A few months prior, my second wife left town with her boyfriend, which left me feeling incredible rejection. I was reeling from her orchestrated betrayal. Shortly after that, the economy and banking institutions began to collapse, bringing financing options for my vocational students to a halt. Still dealing with the emotional and financial aftermath of my wife's action, I had to file for personal and corporate bankruptcy because my business was hemorrhaging cash to cover its overhead. Losing the business I had worked so hard to create filled me with anguish. I was overwhelmed.

I remember receiving the phone call from my ENT that September morning as I sat at my office desk. "Bob, we have your answer. You have cancer."

I was alone, so nobody could hear my quiet sobs or see the tears running down my cheeks. I was both relieved that they figured out that I had squamous cell carcinoma and frightened at the same time. The diagnosis was part three of a 13-month stretch of compounding losses.

I would come to know my ENT as the most genuine, caring, and empathetic physician I would ever meet. No matter how busy or how far behind he was, he would take time at the start of each visit to ask about life and where I had presented my medical myotherapy seminar courses since my last visit. His genuine care was a blessing while I was dealing with my world collapsing around me.

Every six months or so, the cancer would return, and the ENT would cut it out, cauterize it, and send the tissue to the pathologist for evaluation. It always came back as cancer, but I wasn't worried because it was such a slow-growing type. Then, in the late summer of 2013, my recurring tongue pain was different. It wasn't superficial pain anymore. Now, the pain was coming from inside my tongue.

Due to the urgency of this new development, my ENT performed surgery within a week, where he found a fast-growing tumor that was taking over the left side of my tongue. After he closed my tongue up, he told me that he found a tumor that was "half the size of a Tylenol tablet, but wrapped around the nerve that would affect my speech. I was then referred to a renowned surgeon in Seattle who was the top expert in the region on this type of cancer. Knowing I had an aggressive tumor in my tongue was frightening.

I had twenty-three days between my exploratory surgery with my ENT and the next with my Seattle surgeon, and I had much to do. A few days after my surgery with my ENT, I was the keynote speaker for the Thurston County Chamber of Commerce[1]. I was on painkillers. Not so much as to look heavily medicated, but enough to take the edge off of my pain. I admitted to the crowd that I had stitches holding my tongue together when I was speaking. It felt like strings were holding my tongue down. Every word was painful and felt like a tug-of-war when trying to enunciate for clarity.

---

[1] Keynote speech before the Thurston County Chamber of Commerce, September 11, 2013. YouTube: https://youtu.be/FWR64iL-Uic

A few days later, I took my youngest daughter to an all-inclusive resort in Puerto Vallarta, making good on a promise. Years before, I told my girls I would take them on a trip anywhere they wanted to go for at least a week after graduating from high school. Holly chose Mexico.

It was a fun trip and turned out to be more memorable than I had anticipated. One afternoon, we were in the adults-only pool high above the resort pools below. It was sunny, and the poolside attendant served cold beers about as fast as I could drink them. I should have opted for water, especially as I became increasingly dehydrated out in the sun.

The Hilton Puerto Vallarta resort.

At one point, I climbed out of the pool and immediately slipped and fell on the hard, slick marble. I landed on the back of my head and knocked myself unconscious. I was out cold. When I came to, Holly helped me to my feet and walked me back to our room. As she was helping me get into a cold shower, I slipped and fell again, striking my head on the hard tile floor.

The next time I regained consciousness, I was in a Puerto Vallarta hospital emergency room. I remember looking around the room, puzzled. I could have sworn I was in a steam bath. There was so much 'steam,' I thought, not yet realizing it was from the fog that can accompany a serious concussion. Whoops. The lead doctor entered my room and explained that they had performed a CT, MRI, and X-rays. The scans confirmed I had a concussion, but I already knew that. I would later keep my concussion to myself rather than letting the surgeon and anesthesiologist know before my surgery.

In the twelve years between 2001 and 2013, I had been traveling regularly to present my seminars throughout the US. I had never considered what would happen if I lost my ability to speak. Without knowing the outcome of my surgery, I realized that I should get my lecture on video so it could be played to an audience in my absence. I had a plan.

After returning from Mexico and with little time to spare, I set a date for the free lecture and secured a large lecture hall at Evergreen State College in Olympia. Every seat was filled[2] within a few days of sending a few thousand emails to massage therapists and chiropractors in my region. My good friend and college roommate agreed to come up from Portland, Oregon, to handle the recording. Thankfully, the event went off as planned.

---

[2] https://youtu.be/aZxQ-sCJfWQ

The students and guests gathered at the lecture recording session
held in Purce Hall on The Evergreen State College campus.

The day had come for my surgery with my Seattle
surgeon. When I woke up in the recovery area, he said,
"Bob, the tumor was the size of an Oreo cookie, but it's
wrapped around the nerve that lets you talk." Those
were the same words my ENT had said just twenty-
three days earlier. Talk about déjà vu, except for the fact
that the tumor had grown exponentially in just three
weeks.

My surgeon confided, "Bob, we need to take the entire
left half of your tongue." He explained that he would
need to cut it from the tip and all the way back and then
replace it with tissue from my left forearm—a procedure
known as a hemiglossectomy. The tumor was growing
fast. If I wanted to live—which I did—it had to happen
soon. He had given me a heads-up that this was a likely

probability, but nothing prepared me for the punch in the gut when I heard it would actually happen.

As a public speaker and seminar presenter, the thought of potentially losing my ability to speak was beyond frightening. I felt like a baseball pitcher being told he would lose his throwing arm. My voice was a tool that I had honed for most of my adult life and heard by millions in thousands of radio and television commercials, podcasts, and hundreds of hours of educational materials. What would become of me?

In the days leading up to the surgery, I started a video blog to share about what would soon take place. Laying bare your fears is tough, but if I could encourage even one person who would be up against what I was going through, it was worth it. Those videos ultimately resulted in my own encouragement as well through offline dialogues with the audience who had viewed them.

Realizing I likely wouldn't be able to speak intelligibly anytime soon, I had a dilemma. In the coming month, several weeks after my surgery was scheduled, I was to present a large business training at the Washington State Convention Center. That was when I thought I would have a biopsy, not the loss of half of my tongue. Video ads were already playing online and on social media. I had to cancel it, but I had already spent the registration fees I had received on additional advertising, which was my common practice, but I never could have foreseen this. The speakers were scheduled, and the venue was contracted. I couldn't afford to return the registration fees, so I had to be creative and pivot. Pressure seems to breed innovation. With my surgery coming up, I quickly drafted an email to my attendees offering them a refund or a "lifetime membership in a business mentoring group," where they would get all of the training in video format and the ability to get their questions answered. All but one took me up on the latter. That was one less thing to stress about.

The procedure to remove the left half of my tongue took place on October 3, 2013. I spent the first few nights in the intensive care unit (ICU) before being transferred to a private room on an upper floor reserved for cancer patients. Little did I know, the journey that began in 2006 would not just be a fight against cancer but a series of events intent on testing me to my very core.

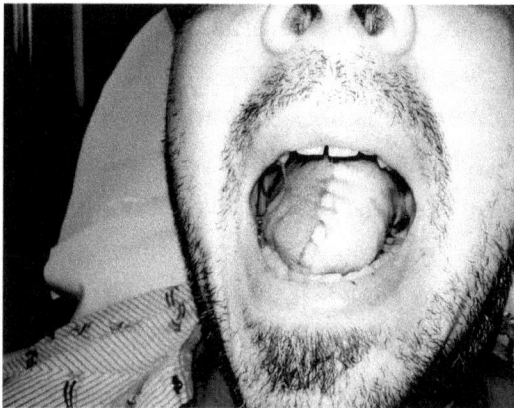

Revealing my tongue after my hemiglossectomy, with my original tongue and the flap from my forearm sewn together with a baseball type of stitch.

As I navigated the uncertainty of my diagnosis and the challenges it brought, I began to realize that my journey wasn't solely about battling a disease; it was about the relationships and responsibilities I had, espe-cially as a parent. I needed to address one of the most difficult aspects of adversity: the importance of being honest with my children.

## Telling Kids the Truth

When I first got diagnosed with tongue cancer in 2008, I was frightened—frightened not just for myself but for my three daughters. I had raised them to be strong and independent but underestimated their emotional fortitude. I was selling them short, thinking my diagnosis would be the one thing they couldn't handle. I was wrong.

It's funny how parents expect nothing short of honesty from their children and promptly punish them when they catch them lying, even lies of omission. We all know lying is wrong. Yet, parents often lie to their children, including half-truths and lies of omission. Parents lie about bad news, like a cancer diagnosis, thinking our children aren't strong enough to handle the truth. They worry that full disclosure about a difficult topic could scare their children because they don't believe they can handle the truth. In reality, children can't handle being lied to, nor the breakdown in trust with their parents. Saying "Everything is going to be okay" when a parent knows it isn't is a breach of trust rather than an opportunity to demonstrate truth in the face of the unknown.

From left, my daughters, Holly, Ashley, and Sara.

I am the proud father of three amazing daughters, Ashley, Sara, and Holly. I love that they each have uniquely different personalities. When I was first diagnosed in 2008, Ashley was living on her own, Sara was in the Netherlands as an exchange student, and Holly, my youngest, was living with me every other week. I was more than nervous but able to talk with Ashley and Holly in person about my cancer diagnosis. I wrestled with burdening Sara with the news. I knew she would wish she could give me a hug and be there for me. I owed her the truth, even if she was 5,000 miles away in Wassenaar, Holland. The day after I told Ashley and Holly, I had that difficult conversation with Sara during our weekly Skype video conference call. Sara thanked me for letting her know and not shielding her from the hard truth.

The hardest part for my three girls was seeing their strong father become weak and fragile during chemo and radiation. At the time, I was 240 pounds of muscle packaged in more fat than I would care to admit, yet I was still a formidable man. Most young children grow up thinking their fathers can do anything. I remember being on the kindergarten playground when I told a friend, "My dad can beat up your dad!" I believed it, although my father wasn't a violent man. In the years since then, I've seen my father slowly transition from a *man of steel* to a man who needs a walker to move about the house, yet still falling regularly. Parents are mortal, though they often think hiding a scary prognosis will keep their children from realizing they aren't mortal after all.

Since wanting to soften my medical prognosis for my girls in 2008, I have endeavored to err on the side of honesty. Keeping the truth from them only served to weaken their trust, but the truth provided them with the opportunity to go through the cancer journey at my side rather than from a distance.

Another important lesson I've learned is that my girls want to know details and updates before I tell others, especially before I announce updates on social media. I've made that mistake several times, and each time I shared an update without telling them first, it caught them off guard, breaking my promise not to do it again.

Recently, I posted an update on Facebook jesting about how I was having a basal cell carcinoma (cancerous mole) removed from my head and how it was a nice distraction from my slowly disintegrating anterior mandible. While I was using 'tongue in cheek' (pun intended) humor, it was the first time my three daughters had heard about the pathology results. They felt diminished and less of a priority. Ugh. I messed up again.

Sharing brutal truths with children and family and supporting people before announcing the news to the world shows them they are important and builds trust that secrets aren't being kept from them.

During my last 12-day inpatient stay in the hospital, my girls took shifts to spend time with me. I wouldn't trade that time with them for anything in the world, as it gave us chances to talk, share about life, laugh, and cry together. Even when the truth is scary, it can be incredibly liberating.

Talking with my daughters about my diagnosis was a necessary step, but it made me curious about how others in my family, especially my mother, had experienced this journey. Her perspective offered a different insight into the impact of my struggles.

## Through the Eyes of My Mother

I have been blessed to have parents who've always supported me and my decisions. They've offered wisdom when I've needed it, and most importantly, they have been a powerhouse of encouragement. I attribute my successes in life to their encouraging words. Even when I lost my business and my home during The Great Recession, they spoke life to me with words of encouragement and prayed for me every day.

While I knew my experiences affected me, I hadn't given much thought to how my cancer journey affected my family. It wasn't until I started writing this book that I asked my mother how my difficult journey with cancer affected her. She answered with the following letter.

**Thoughts from my 91-year-old mother:**

*When my son first told me he had cancer, my world fell apart. I couldn't believe it was him and not me. It felt so unfair. Why didn't I get it instead? I kept thinking, "It should have been me." As his mother, I would have gladly taken on that burden to spare him from it. I felt so angry at God for letting this happen and so incredibly sad, almost like I was in a nightmare I couldn't wake up from. The pain of knowing my son was suffering was unlike anything I had ever experienced before. There was a constant ache in my heart that wouldn't go away.*

*I wanted to take the cancer from him and go through the pain myself, like any mother would for her child. It was all I could think about. I would have given anything to make it go away. But instead, I felt helpless, which was one of the hardest parts. I was his mom, the one who always kissed his scraped knees and comforted him when he was scared, the one who was supposed to be able to make things better. But now, I couldn't protect him from something so big and so scary. All I could do was be there for him as much as possible and try to give him strength, even though I felt like I was falling apart inside.*

*Bob was living on his own when he had his first cancer surgery. I remember feeling frustrated because I couldn't be there with him all the time. I wanted to be by his side every minute, holding his hand and telling him it was going to be okay, but I couldn't. He was an adult, trying to maintain some independence, even through all of this. I admired him for that, but it also broke my heart. I wanted to do more, but I did what I could. I remember thinking about what small things I could do to make him feel just a little better. I knew he loved milkshakes from Baskin & Robbins—chocolate fudge ice cream, malt, and hot fudge—so after each of his surgeries, his dad and I brought him one. It wasn't much, but I hoped it gave him some comfort. I always worried that he wasn't getting enough to eat since he couldn't have solid food for days, so we always brought him the biggest shake they had, hoping it would help him feel better. It may have just been a milkshake, but to us, it was the one thing we could do to show our love and care when everything else seemed out of our hands.*

*There were so many moments when I wished I could do more. I remember sitting by Bob's bedside, looking at him, and thinking how unfair it all was. He was so young, and he had so much life ahead of him. It wasn't supposed to be like this. But through it all, Bob never complained. Watching my son go through so many surgeries on his tongue was heartbreaking, but it also made me so proud. He faced each procedure with such bravery, even though I knew how much pain he was in. He never complained, not even once. He faced everything with a strength I always knew he had but had never seen so clearly. It was like every bit of his character, courage, and resilience came to the surface, shining so brightly. I couldn't have been prouder.*

*Somehow, even though he was the one suffering, he helped me, his family, and his friends through it all. I don't know how he did it. He would smile at us, crack a joke, or just tell us that everything was going to be okay, and it lifted us up. He was the one who needed comforting, but instead, he was the one giving comfort. He showed us what real courage looks like, and for that, I will always be grateful. I learned so much from my son during that time—about strength, about resilience, and about love. He showed me that even in the darkest of times, there can be light. Even when things seem impossible, there is still hope. And as his mother, I couldn't be prouder of the person he is. His courage and strength are things I will carry with me for the rest of my life, and I hope others see it, too. He is truly an inspiration, not just to me but to everyone who knows him.*

Reading my mother's reflections reminded me that adversity will shape not only our present but also our future. Although patterns of hardship emerged from my past, they would repeat themselves in ways I couldn't yet anticipate, bringing a familiar yet daunting sense of déjà vu.

# Déjà Vu: When Adversity Repeats Itself

## "We can be 'cancer-free,' but never be free of cancer."

Those words were spoken to me by my friend, Dr. Cobie Whitten, a Psycho-Oncology Consultant. She explained that the worry and concern of a recurrence are always in the back of our minds. She wasn't wrong, but I did my best not to dwell on things that *could* happen. After losing the left half of my tongue and dozens of lymph nodes on October 3, 2013, I was declared "cancer-free" and told the chemotherapy would extend my life by another ten years. The decade of life extension was a gift, but it felt a little like a ticking timebomb that would blow my life up and likely take my life in exchange for those 'bonus' years.

Following my recovery from treatment, I jumped back into my seminar business. I kicked back into high gear, scheduling convention centers and hotel ballrooms for my courses across the country, spanning from the East Coast to Waikiki Beach, Hawaii, and a dozen more in between. I taught two weekends a month for nine months every year and vacationed as much as possible for the other three months. In his book, *The 4-Hour Workweek*, Timothy Ferris encourages his readers to live like they're retired while they still have their health, and that's exactly what I did. Even with only half of my tongue, my seminar business was going great, and I even remarried in 2015.

In the late summer of 2019, my new wife and I spent a couple of weeks in Europe in the middle of a heat wave. Then, we spent the second week of January in Las Vegas to attend the CES, the Consumer Electronics Show, with 171,000 of our 'closest friends' from around the globe. CES can best be described as an aggregation of the largest convention center halls in the world—halls filled with shoulder-to-shoulder attendees working their way through thousands of product booths sprawled over several properties nearby. Over 11,000 of those attendees had flown in from China. This was in January of 2020 in facilities where we were all breathing in the same air the next person was exhaling. The COVID pandemic was underway.

We flew home for a few days and then to a resort in Loreto, Mexico. Shortly after arriving, I started getting painful spasms in my neck. After all of my cancer surgery history, I can take pain, but these spasms? The pain was off the chart. The waves of spasms were intense and unrelenting. We took a shuttle into town for lunch between waves of pain before walking through the gift shops. As we walked down the street, we passed by a neighborhood hospital. My neck muscles seized again—even more intensely than before. I looked at my wife as I was grabbing my neck and said, "I need to see a doctor." The pain from the spasms grew with increasing intensity.

The hospital was small and sparse in design, but what it lacked in fancy decor, it made up for it with a large staff. Within minutes, I was ushered back into the main patient treatment room. Several doctors were attending to me, performing manual tests and scans, ultimately sending me on my way with a bottle of muscle relaxants and a bottle of painkillers. Since they wouldn't directly invoice my health insurance for the costs, I was a little nervous asking what I owed them. The statement of charges totaled less than $100.

I went to the local ER twice in two days. One of the resort doctors even visited our suite several times before he said I should see my doctors in Washington State to find out what was wrong.

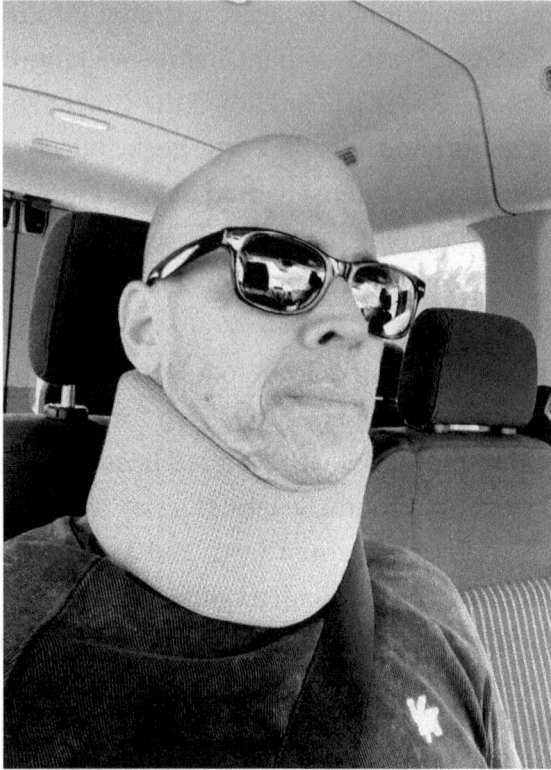

In the airport transfer van for my return flight to Seattle.

My wife called for her assistant to pick me up at the SeaTac airport and drive me directly to an emergency room in Olympia. As I was being transferred by wheelchair to my gate at the Mexican airport, my wife posted photos of herself by the pool. I felt that familiar feeling of abandonment and rejection. Her decision not to return with me was an omen of what lay ahead. She filed for divorce a short time later.

Once I arrived at the hospital in Olympia, the attending physician looked at the images he had ordered of my neck and chest scans and said, "Mr. Haase..." He paused for a moment, searching for the right words. "Your lungs look... odd." The closest thing he could compare it to was 'valley fever,' which would later be determined to look a lot like COVID-19, but the hospital hadn't seen any of those cases yet. My blood pressure was at 270/150. Although COVID tests weren't available until over a month later, it doesn't take a lot of reasoning to think that I was one of the first cases in Washington State. A month later, Washington Governor Jay Inslee declared a state of emergency, and within two months, most other states had followed. After losing my business a decade before, I was getting a pit in my stomach, a feeling that a business upheaval was ahead.

I had been working to expand my seminar business in the months preceding the pandemic. The goal was to select some of my best students and train them to teach my courses across the US with a unique licensing program. Being an excellent medical massage therapist does not mean the therapist can teach, so I asked the potential instructors to send me a video of themselves teaching me *anything*. Even a video of 'how to make a grilled cheese sandwich,' which two of them did. The results were humorous, but they gave me insights into how each might perform in an educational setting.

Several months after starting my search, I had my team of six instructors licensed to present my courses in 42 of the 50 states. In the training program, each instructor learned how to secure teaching venues in their regions and how to register students for their seminars. Everything was going according to plan until January 2020, when I got a call from my contact at the Washington State Convention Center. "Bob, we are seeing the start of a trend. This COVID-19 virus is causing event planners to cancel their events. I just wanted to give you a heads-up."

Sure enough, venues across the country began canceling in-person events. Within a couple of weeks, all of the seminars scheduled for my new team of instructors were immediately canceled, leaving us all without work. I was in shock. Months of planning and training. Countless hours of automated system configurations. All of it for naught. My newly-trained instructors were also caught off guard after reconfiguring their businesses so they could present my courses. It knocked the wind out of my emotional sails.

A year and a half later, the state of emergency in Washington was finally lifted. By then, I had been un-employed and living off the economic stimulus and COVID relief fund the federal government was deposit-ing into my checking account.

I eventually came to realize that things would never be the same. Meanwhile, I worked quickly to finish my first book on facing adversity, *Not What You Had Planned: Finding Strength and Hope in the Storms of Adversity.* Even as that book was published in the summer of 2020, I could have never conceived of the challenges lying in wait for me.

Trying to apply for jobs with my resume took a decrypter with a cipher ring. What did I do for a living? *Everything.* I worked alone, except for my seminar assistants, whom I would fly to each seminar destination. I was responsible for securing and contracting venues, designing direct mail pieces, and producing instruction manuals. Again, thanks to Tim Ferris, I learned to automate many of the tasks I used to pay a secretary to handle. So, how does that translate to a resume? And how old do I sound when an online application asks how many years of experience I have using Photoshop? Answer: Over thirty.

After my frustration peaked, I decided to do what I did best: make a video. A *video resume* is probably a better description. I set up a backdrop in the family room, arranged the studio lights, set the camera and tripod, put on my suit, and then told my story, detailing my experience, skills, and why my speech was somewhat different.

I had nothing to lose. I posted the video[3] to LinkedIn and Facebook, and a few weeks later, I started my new job as a Director of Communications for a statewide

---

[3] https://youtu.be/e_Q95pHQfcM

association. It was more than ironic. I landed a great communications job with only half of a tongue. I was truly blessed.

Several of my "friends" on Facebook were news reporters, and after seeing my posts about my story in 2013, one of them was able to get in touch with my daughter Ashley to see if I was up for an interview regarding my journey. The story[4] ran on NBC's local affiliate, KING5 News in Seattle, while I was in the ICU and another story the following June while I was teaching a business seminar in Bellevue, Washington, which was also covered in the USA Today[5], as well as several other newspapers and organizations. Seattle's ABC station, KOMO4, also ran a follow-up story[6] in July of 2015. Fast forward to the early summer of 2023.

I was looking forward to sharing with the Seattle news affiliates a 'feel good'/'where is he now' story of my ten-year journey with half of my tongue, and thanks to my job, I had over two dozen reporters in my contacts. But in July of that year, I started feeling a sharp edge on the back of my front lower teeth. The friction slowly worsened, eventually causing my tongue to bleed, making speech painful.

---

[4] https://youtu.be/9l6IPZ3dLj8
[5] https://www.usatoday.com/story/news/2014/06/18/inspiration-nation-motivational-speaker-loses-tongue/10760365
[6] http://youtu.be/bDcOVBRKd9w

I had my dentist grind down and smooth the backs of the offending teeth, but it didn't help. Nothing changed except the look of my tongue. The color was bluish, almost like it was slightly bruised.

Next, I met with Kaiser's new ENT. He didn't see anything abnormal without a reference point of what my tongue looked or felt like before the changes. Something was wrong, though. I could feel it.

My Seattle surgeon got me in immediately. I met with him at his office on August 9. He could tell that things weren't right, too, ordering a priority CT scan for August 12. Just after my morning scan, I returned home, and as I exited my car, I felt a gooey ball of phlegm in my mouth and spit it out into the bushes next to my garage. It wasn't phlegm. Instead, a large glob of red goo, the size and consistency of a small egg yolk, landed on the bush.

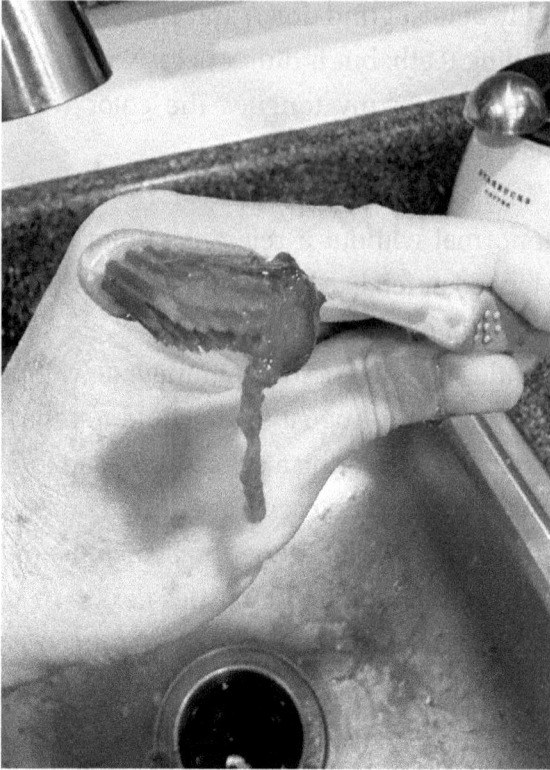

String-like tissue purged from my tongue on August 12, 2023.

I ran inside after immediately feeling another glob form and then another. For the next 30 minutes, my tongue was purging various forms of stringy tissue and gelatinized blood. My bathroom sink looked like the scene of a murder. In total, the ejected contents were nearly the equivalent volume of my visible tongue. What I was seeing was unreal. Blood coming from a tongue? Sure. But chunks of bloody debris? Never in my life. This was the stuff of horror films.

As gross as it sounds, I took photos and videos of the types of tissue lying in the sink. I felt like I should document what I was seeing because it was surreal.

I needed to see a doctor, so I called a lifelong friend who lived 10 minutes away. "Kristi? Can you drive me to Urgent Care? I shouldn't drive." I didn't know if a subsequent purge was coming. Less than half an hour later, Kristi walked me into the Urgent Care clinic, which stood not 50 feet from where I had my CT scan earlier that morning. Thankfully, the bloody purging had stopped by then.

At the check-in counter, I told the receptionist that I had been bleeding from my mouth and even had "chunks" purging from my tongue. I figured the more graphical I could be, the faster I would get to see a doctor. Sure enough, no less than two minutes after I had found a seat in the waiting area, my name was called.

The triage nurse brought me back into the triage area and asked me to give her more information about what had happened. As I started to explain, her eyes widened.

Usually, patients would be told to have a seat and then call you when it was your turn. Instead, the nurse stood up from her exam stool and said, "Follow me." I followed her down the hall to a curtained-off exam room, where she told me to take a seat. No sooner had I sat down than a nurse came in to take my blood pressure and ask additional medical history questions. When she asked what had happened, I told her it would be easier to show her, and I pulled my iPhone out of my pocket. Her eyes widened as well, and she left to fetch the doctor. I guessed she was a bit alarmed when she talked to him because less than a minute had passed before the attending physician walked in.

"What seems to be going on, Mr. Haase?" After a brief explanation, he grabbed a wooden tongue depressor and turned on his visor 'headlight' to get a better look at my unusual anatomy. "It's kind of a 'war zone' in there, eh, doc?" By the time the doctor inspected my mouth, the bloody purge had stopped, so he couldn't see any evidence of what I had described taking place less than an hour earlier. "I'm not really seeing anything," he said as he pulled out the depressor and sat back. "I think you need to see this," I said with a bit of a smirk. I pulled out my phone and flipped through the images and video. His eyes widened, and he had a faint look of horror that he was trying to conceal. "Um... I'll be right back. I need to look into this," he said as he left my curtained room.

The truth is, emergency room and urgent care center doctors see a lot of lacerations, broken bones, and other types of bloody injuries, but an erupting tongue? Not so much.

Twenty minutes passed, and he hadn't yet returned, so I poked my head out and saw him speaking with someone on the phone with his hand on his head. When he eventually returned, the doctor told me he had contacted my surgeon and discussed what he saw on my phone. With the CT scan results expedited, my surgeon was able to see the tale-tell signs of a tumor in my tongue and put in a rush order for a PET scan to take place on Monday, two days later.

The expedited pathology report confirmed that the cancer had returned to my tongue.

My surgeon, Dr. Steven Bayles, explained in his usual calm voice, "We need to take your entire tongue, Bob. It's called a total glossectomy. The tumor is two inches long and reaches to the roots of your front lower teeth." Even though the delivery of the cancer diagnosis was gentle, it still felt like a sudden punch to my gut—the kind that left me unable to breathe. I felt numb, trying to make sense of what he was saying. I couldn't help but think about the road ahead.

I have thought about the worst-case scenario of losing my entire tongue over the years. I had compartmentalized it, though, shoving it into the back recesses of my mind. As a business owner, I would always plan for calamity and hope for the best. Still, no business downturn would ever compare to the surreal suggestion of losing my ability to speak. I tried not to think about it, but how could I not? I was the guy who loved to use his voice to entertain, educate, and encourage people, whether it be an audience of one or 1,000.

I've spent decades honing my craft of speaking in different environments. I loved looking into each audience member's eyes to get a read on their response to my message in real-time. The bigger the group, the better. I think well on my feet and love answering questions with stories and analogies to make my point in a congenial way. Suddenly, being forced to come to terms with the fact that those days were over was incomprehensibly unfathomable. Wanting to stay strong, or at least *appear* strong, was difficult in the days leading up to the surgery.

Even as I worked to rebuild my life, the signs of another challenge were becoming clear. It was time to once again trust the expertise of my medical team and prepare for what was to come.

## Into the Hands of the Surgeons

In the days leading up to the surgery, I took time to record multiple personal messages for my family, so should they ever want to hear my voice again, they would have the recorded audio file to listen to. Those recordings were tough. I failed miserably at keeping my emotions in check, trying to suppress my tears. My voice quivered as I knew these words would be some of my last. While recording, I couldn't help but wonder why this was happening again.

Dr. Bayles organized two specialized surgical teams to complete the removal of my tongue and the subsequent placement of the flap[7]. The grueling 6-hour procedure was scheduled for August 28, 2023. Bayles explained how he would need to cut out the previous flap and the rest of my original tongue. He would also need to pull all the lower teeth and create an entirely new flap to allow me to swallow. This would be a significant flap. To build

---

[7] A 'flap' refers to a piece of tissue that's transferred from one part of the body to another along with its blood supply. The original flap to replace half of my tongue was taken from my left forearm.

it, they would need to remove one of the four 'quad' muscles in my right leg. The entire muscle, running from my hip to my knee.

## It was time

My oldest daughter, Ashley, and middle daughter, Sara, planned to drive me to the surgery early in the morning on August 28. Those who know my girls know they love to make me cry by writing sentimental messages on my birthday and Father's Day cards. They also look for ways to make me laugh when I'm down. The night before was no different. After an evening of talking and laughing, going to bed was bittersweet.

Ashley and Sara drove me to the surgery center from Kirkland, Washington, and across the I-90 floating bridge the next morning. We arrived at the check-in desk just after 7:00 a.m. It felt a little ominous as the check-in desk and family waiting areas were vacant except for the three of us.

A decade earlier, my family was allowed, one at a time, to go back and visit with me in the surgery prep area. However, thanks to COVID-19, hospitals tightened up their policies. When the check-in reception person told them about the change, it didn't sit well with my girls, and the time before I would be taken back increased the urgency they felt before I would be taken away.

I hugged and kissed my girls one last time before being taken to the prep area. We were all in tears, knowing we had to say our goodbyes and that I had likely spoken some of the last intelligible words my girls would ever hear from me. "I love you, Ashley. I love you, Sara. See you soon."

After I was out of sight, Ashley and Sara went out for breakfast before Ashley was picked up by her husband on their way to Eastern Washington. Sara was left alone to wait. She was told the surgery would last only six hours—it lasted nine. Worried and alone after nine hours, she finally received a call that the surgery was over, and I was on my way to recovery before being transferred to a room upstairs. "I'll call you back when you can come see your father," the nurse said in an assuring voice. More than an hour had passed when Sara finally got the call for her to come see me in the ICU.

When she entered the room, five of the surgical team encircled my bed, talking quickly and actively doing something, but nothing was clear as to what was happening. Seeing Sara, one of the team members approached her and spoke quietly, just inches from her face. "We're having difficulty with the 'flap' in his mouth, the one we constructed from his leg muscle," the doctor whispered. "The problem is, we can't hear a pulse in the flap. The situation is changing in real-time, and we may have to take your dad back into surgery tonight if we can't get a pulse." It was then that the lead surgeon was called to come and make a first-hand assessment.

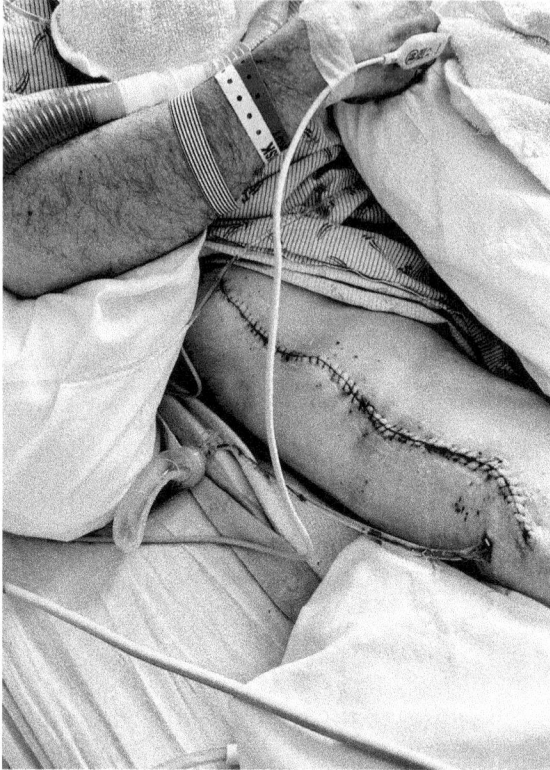

Showing the scar on my right thigh where the surgeon removed one of my quad muscles to rebuild a 'flap' to replace my tongue.

Sara would later describe to me what she saw.

*"Your whole body was shaking. You were in severe pain and in shock but happy to see me, even though you couldn't really smile. Blood was on the wall. I'm not sure how it got there, but your drain tubes were full of red goo. Things were messy, and you looked a bit like Frankenstein.*

40

*Your neck was cut from ear to ear, drain tubes were coming out everywhere, and you had wicked-long stitches on your leg from your knee to your hip. Surprisingly, your face looked good because the inflammation hadn't yet settled in. There were too many people all up in your space, so I held your feet like you would someone's hand, and it seemed to help you stop shaking,"* Sara explained.

*"The staff were asking you yes/no questions, checking to get a sense of your cognitive abilities. When the hospital staff asked you questions, you used your fingers to signify numbers, or you would scribble on a dry-erase whiteboard they gave you. You explained how you and I had worked together in your medical myotherapy seminars and that we were okay with 'medical speak.' You scribbled words on your board, and I filled in the blanks of what you were trying to say."*

By the third day, Sara said my handwriting had improved, but it looked like 'hieroglyphs' because I was still shaking. Sara continued,

*"When you were made aware of the tongue flap blood supply concern and the potential of another surgery, you panicked a bit. Your heart rate skyrocketed. You were also upset when you*

*realized how large of a chunk they cut out of your thigh. You weren't very happy about that. I asked for a blanket so you'd stop fixating on your leg scar and meds to relieve your pain and calm you down. Once they sorted out the blood supply concern, they gave you enough pain meds to let you drift off to sleep."*

Although they took me back for surgery at 7:30 AM that morning, it wasn't until 11:30 PM that Sara was finally able to head home so she could rest.

Sara arrived just before 8:00 AM the next morning to keep me company and entertained for the day. I was in the process of slowly waking up from the fog of medications and the trauma of surgery—and I was *hungry*. It had been 36 hours since I last ate. I used my writing board to communicate I needed something to settle my growing hunger pangs. Sara pushed my call button, and the nurse arrived a few minutes later. Sara inquired about me getting fed, and the nurse said the food pump should arrive shortly.

Hours had passed, but no pump. With a tone growing increasingly tenacious, Sara said to the nurse, *"My dad needs food."* When the nurse got to the point, the feeding machine was delivered within the hour, and the formula bag was hooked up and ready for its slow journey into the nasogastric (NG) tube that had been placed through my nose and down into my stomach during surgery. There was just one problem, though. The formula wasn't moving. Sara pressed the call button once again, and this time, the nurse determined that the tube was kinked somewhere on its way to my stomach and a specialist would need to come and 'unkink' it.

The nutrition nurse spent a good deal of time trying to get the tube working. I could tell something wasn't right. Eventually, she said, "Mr. Haase, the tube is kinked along the abdominal wall. I'm sorry, but it isn't going to work for us. We will need to wait until later tomorrow afternoon to feed you once your abdominal PEG tube is installed."

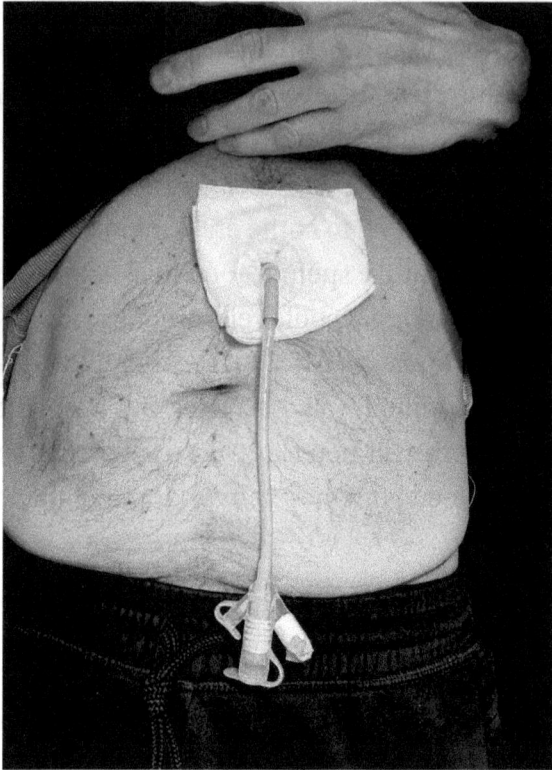

My permanent abdominal PEG tube for formula feeding.

Choosing a three-day fast is one thing, but being forced to forego food for three days is another. Late in the afternoon the following day, my PEG tube was placed, and I was moved up to the 16th floor. My stomach was finally feeling better, even if I was only receiving flavorless tan-colored liquid from a bottle.

After the commotion of settling me into my private patient room and the lights were dimmed, I closed my eyes in hopes of getting some sleep. It was time to let the healing begin.

Sara's unwavering support during my surgery was just the beginning; the next twelve days at the hospital would test my resilience and the strength of those who stood by my side.

When a Facebook friend later saw the scar on one of my posts, he asked, "Bro, how long is your new tongue??" That made me chuckle. I envisioned a cartoon character whose tongue would unroll like a licorice wheel. The important thing about the flap is that even though I can't feel it, I wouldn't be able to swallow without it.

How I envisioned my tongue to appear after seeing my long leg scar.
Created with DALL·E, OpenAI's image generation tool.

While I experienced the surgery firsthand, the impact extended far beyond me. My daughter Sara, who had been by my side through so much of this journey, had her own perspective on what unfolded—a view shaped by both love and resilience.

## Sara's View

Over the past decade, my middle daughter, Sara, has spent the most time with me, especially after 2015, when my seminar teaching assistant of nine years tragically passed away during a sporting event. Sara stepped in and began traveling with me across the country, from Miami to Anchorage, Honolulu, and countless cities in between. Eventually, she was promoted in her own career and had to step away from teaching with me, but she has always stayed connected—whether through FaceTime calls or visiting me in the hospital, just across Lake Washington from her home.

Recently, I asked Sara if she could share some thoughts about how my cancer journey has impacted her, and she shared this:

> *When I think about how my dad's cancer journey has impacted me, I can't help but realize how much I take for granted. Watching him lose the ability to speak and eat—things most of us never even think about—is such a reality check. It's made me stop and appreciate how much easier I have it. Emotionally, though, I'm at a loss. I can't even put into words how I feel, and honestly, I think that's because I'm avoiding it. I just don't have the energy to dig that deep right now. Instead, I take things one day, one appointment, one update at a time so I can stay focused and be there when my dad needs me.*
>
> *This whole journey has been both devastating and incredible. Incredible because my dad is literally beating the odds every day. He has his tough moments, physically and emotionally, but he always tries to focus on the good. I think it's*

*his way of helping the rest of us do the same. It reminds me of a long-running disaster movie that keeps getting sequels nobody asked for. It started back in 2008, stopped for a bit, then rebooted again and again. At this point, I'm like, "Seriously? We're still doing this?" But the main character is someone I love, so I keep showing up.*

*For me, staying grounded has been all about finding balance. I've learned to set boundaries and not obsess over what I can't control. Humor has been my coping mechanism. Turning the sad moments into dark little comedy skits in my head helps keep me sane. And I've made it a point to take care of myself because if I'm not okay, I can't be there for my dad when things get heavy. It's like refueling for when the skits evolve into full-blown feature films.*

*As hard as this has been, it's brought me and my dad closer. He's always been open with me, but cancer has taken it to another level. There are times when I can't give him the reassurance he needs. I can't pretend everything's going to be fine. All I can do is be there with him in the tough moments and remind myself how precious each day is. The biggest gift in all of this has been the bond we've built. And yeah, even though the 2008 disaster movie rebooted again in 2023, I've*

*signed on for the ride, happily sticking by his side
until the credits roll.*

Sara's reflections highlighted the emotional weight carried by those who supported me. Her presence during my recovery became even more vital during the twelve long days I spent in the hospital—days that tested not only my endurance but the strength of those who stood by my side.

# 12 Days in the Hospital

If you have ever spent a couple of weeks confined to a hospital room, you would probably agree that it isn't highly recommended. I think spending the entire day and night confined to a hospital bed or the adjacent guest chair would be best compared to prison confinement. For an active person, the stay almost feels tortuous.

My postural aches and pains at my age require at least six pillows to get comfortable, likely five more than I would get in prison, so that was a plus. With the nurses constantly measuring my urine output and praising me when I did well, I felt like the family dog who peed where I was supposed to when they would say, "Yay! That's great!" It's like when my iWatch praises me for standing up once an hour when it says, "You did it! You've earned an hour toward your stand goal!"

There were *so many* specialists stopping by around the clock. At one point, I had three different specialists stop by simultaneously. It was nuts. They were gracious to each other, though, backing out and waiting for their turns *unless* a doctor entered, which is when everyone else would quietly back out of my room until the doctor was finished.

As it was a teaching hospital, doctors working on their ENT residency followed my doctor into my room. They encircled my bed when it was time to check in on me. The surgeon's biggest concern was ensuring the pulse in my new flap was functioning. They would take a cotton swab on a stick and poke the flap to observe how quickly it would flush from white back to red. Then, they would use an audio-only ultrasound to listen for blood flow. Each time the doctor would press it in just the right spot, the speaker emitted a swooshing noise that sounded like an ultrasound listening to a baby in the womb.

Since all patients who have surgeries similar to mine end up with extensive swelling in their throats and necks, the surgical team preemptively performed a tracheotomy on me where they cut a hole in my neck just above my chest bone and inserted a "trach" tube so I could breathe.

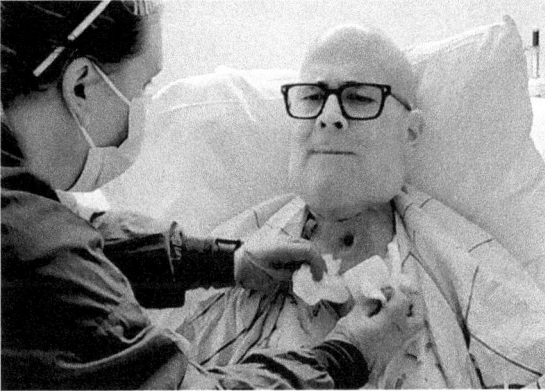

The respiratory therapist changed the dressing surrounding the 'stoma' (hole) for my tracheotomy.

The respiratory therapists were the most frequent visitors to my room day and night. They were tasked with changing my goo-saturated dressings and helping me eject fluids from the hole in my neck so I could breathe. It was disgusting for me, but they always remained calm and reassuring, even when I would occasionally be in distress because I couldn't get enough oxygen into my lungs. After they finished cleaning me up and assured me I could breathe without restrictions, they would apply fresh dressings and be on their way.

Shift nurses were in charge of my meds, asking me to hold up my fingers to signify my level of pain on a 0-10 scale. They would grind up the oxycodone pills along with alternating doses of Tylenol and Advil, add some water, and then squirt them into my feeding tube.

My body was still reeling from the extensive surgery. My mouth and throat continued to swell from the removal of my tongue and sixteen lower teeth, my belly hurt from the PEG tube install, I had no strength in my neck after being cut 'from ear to ear,' and my right thigh was painful and weak. Standing up was a painful exercise, thanks to having one of my long thigh muscles in my leg removed. Even with the pain, I felt cooped up. I wanted to get moving.

In the corner of my room was a folded-up walker. Thanks to watching my nurses turn off the alarms when I needed to use the restroom, I had a plan. I put on a fresh pair of hospital-issued non-slip socks (a must for those they deemed likely to fall), unplugged my IV, oxygen monitor, and feeding tube machines, silenced the alarms, grabbed the walker, and started down the hall. I smiled as I passed the nurses' station. They would have no idea I shouldn't be walking about if I looked confident. At least, that was my plan, and it worked! I figured, 'better to ask for forgiveness than permission,' right?

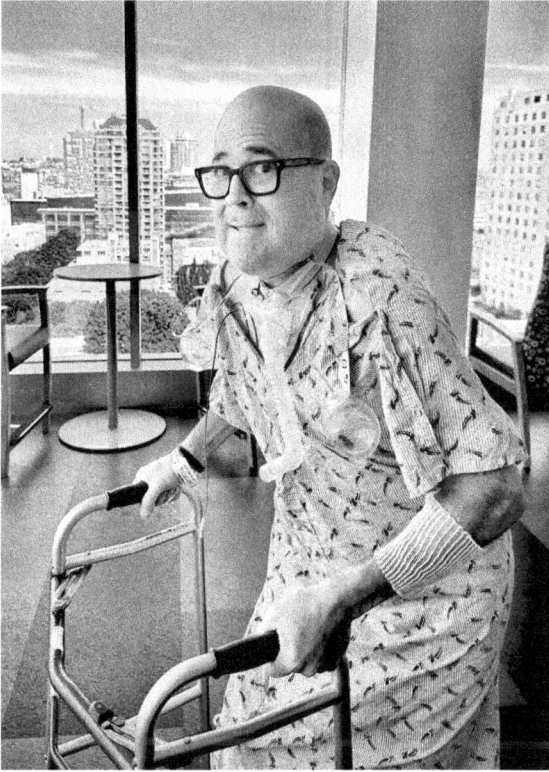

On the loose in the hospital's cancer wing.

My unsupervised walk must have triggered something because I got a visit from the physical therapist the
next day. She was memorable from the minute she
arrived. The best way to describe her is to say that she
was a morph between a high school gym teacher, an
Army drill sergeant, and a standup comedian who
moonlit as a tour guide, repeating the same jokes she
had said a million times before. She brought some fun

to my day and helped offset my feeling of getting stir-crazy with hospital/cabin fever.

After I had been in the hospital for a few days, a nurse's assistant came to my room in the late morning and said she needed to give me a sponge bath. After a brief discussion, she agreed to leave me an assortment of personal cleansing and grooming items necessary for me to do most of the work and return later to scrub my back for me. My favorite were these thick cleansing cloths that were packaged like baby wipes. She even warmed them up for me. She told me to push my call light so she could return to finish up and help me into fresh hospital pajamas and robe. Even though I did most of the work, it felt odd to depend on someone else to get cleaned up.

After the assistant left the room, I disrobed and walked over to my hospital room sink to shave. Seeing myself in the mirror above was tough. My neck had been cut, nearly ear to ear, to give the surgeons access to work inside my mouth, leaving it looking like a throat cut in a horror movie. Drain tubes seemed to come out everywhere, including the sides of my neck and my collarbones, each emptying into collection bottles full of what looked like watered-down Pepto Bismol. I felt grotesque and repulsive. That face wasn't mine. I even had a new off-center dimple in my chin.

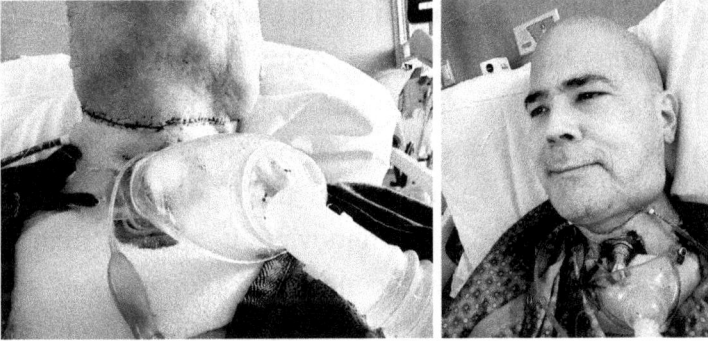

Showing how my neck was cut from ear to ear with bilateral drain tubes.

Over the next few days, my jaws grew more prominent—almost cartoonish. The swelling disfigured my face, and I began to feel like the father character in the American Dad cartoon. At least I had a 'strong' jawline.

Three months apart. Left, taken in June 2023; right, taken in September 2023 while still in the hospital.

In 2013, my tracheotomy tube was in place just for the 12 days I was in the hospital and then removed just before being discharged from the hospital. This time, however—a decade later—no such luck. When the doctor pulled the trach tube that was protruding from the center hole in my neck, I couldn't breathe. Not good. The lead surgeon was summoned to give her opinion and said, "Bob, we can't send you home if you cannot breathe. I want to leave it in place for another four months before we try removing it again. 'Great,' I thought. I knew how inconvenient and unsightly the tube would be and how it would feel like I was drowning if any water got into the hole in my neck when showering.

Getting through the seemingly endless days of monotony and stress took work. Although the hospital had free Wi-Fi, I could only watch so much Netflix before going nuts. It helped me to take time to journal my thoughts, pray, scribble down ideas of what I would paint next, and read. My girls and friends took time in shifts to be with me during visiting hours so I wouldn't be alone. The hospital had given me a small white dry-erase board to use when I woke up from my surgery. That board was my communication lifeline to my doctors, nurses, therapists, family, and friends. Without it, I would have been emotionally isolated—even more than I already was. Focusing on my blessings and keeping myself distracted were my lifelines.

As I write this, over a year later, my airflow remains restricted to a narrow opening in my trachea, leaving me to breathe through what feels like a straw.

Overall, this surgical ordeal seemed less intense compared to my major surgery a decade earlier. While I was in the ICU following my first surgery, I had a panic attack one night when my '1/2 tongue, half flap' had swollen so much the stitches broke, and my 'tongue' was protruding a couple of inches out of my mouth. My jaw was locking because it had to stretch more than ever. But this time was different in many ways. I wasn't as fearful—probably because it 'wasn't my first rodeo—yet I was more stressed, still grappling with the reality that I would never speak again.

Leaving the hospital was a relief, but the physical changes I faced were profound. Each day brought new adjustments and challenges as I learned to live with the visible reminders of my journey.

# PART TWO

## WAVES OF CHANGE

PART TWO

## Feeling Like Frankenstein

When I look in the mirror, I barely recognize the person staring back. I see the long sperm-shaped scar on my left forearm from my surgery in 2013 and the long scar on my right leg that now has a noticeably smaller circumference. I see the feeding tube dangling from my abdomen, the scars on my neck, and my lower lip shriveling and unable to close against my upper lip enough to keep me from drooling. If I ever considered myself an attractive man, those days are gone. I would love to have my younger, more muscular body back, but that isn't possible.

Post-surgery, the hospital's cancer team/tumor board concluded I should only receive radiation without chemotherapy. Two radiation treatments a day for 25 days, for a total of 50. I was told I was being given a 'lifetime maximum' of radiation in 2013, leaving me to wonder about the risks of undergoing 50 additional treatments a decade later. What could go wrong? I shouldn't have wondered. Too much radiation typically leads to cancer, yet it is used to save lives. Too much can also lead to 'osteonecrosis' of the affected area, also known as bone death. My lower anterior mandible (front of my jaw and chin bone) lost blood flow. The bone was dying and continued to deteriorate. Even after (40) 90-minute hyperbaric pressure treatments, the bone remains in a slow process of disintegrating. Hopefully, by the time I need a jaw replacement, someone will have figured out how to create a new jaw bone with a medical 3D printer.

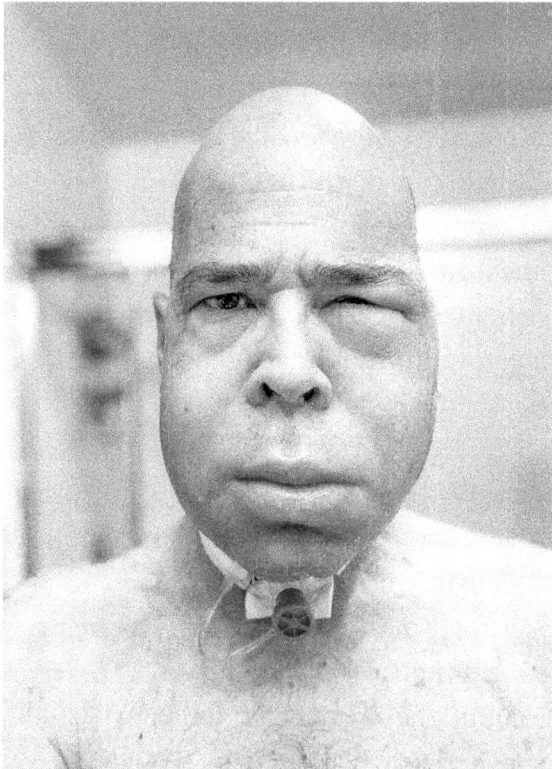

Cellulitis infection, November 2023

Shortly after my 50th radiation treatment, I woke up in the morning with a face that was disfigured and swollen. I had contracted a dangerous cellulitis[8] infection, which was eventually subdued by antibiotics. Then, it was back just a couple of days after completing the treatment. The Urgent Care doctor then put me on Augmentin, a potent antibiotic, which again cleared me of infection, only for it to return just days later. It seems the necrotic bone was the culprit, and until it heals someday, I'll be on a perpetual twice-a-day regimen of the medication.

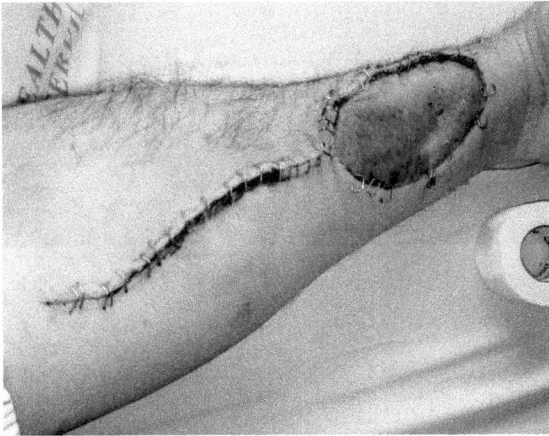

The oddly-shaped scar on my left forearm after
the original flap surgery in the fall of 2013

The changes to my body, daily life, and relationships have been staggering. These are just a few of the physical changes:

8  https://www.mayoclinic.org/diseases-conditions/cellulitis/symptoms-causes/syc-20370762

- **I can no longer speak intelligibly**. Most people can't understand me and have no clue what I am trying to say, while a minority can, for the most part. It sounds like nonsense to the casual observer.

- **My legs are imbalanced**. It turns out that removing an entire muscle, 25% of my right leg's quadriceps muscle, makes exercise tricky and unstable. I once had powerful, muscular legs, but now they are both weak.

- **I can no longer eat food** and instead rely on pouring flavorless formula and protein powder into the 8.5" tube dangling from my belly. I can no longer take part in enjoying a meal with friends or tasting cookies at a company Christmas party.

- **I have to plug my nose** to create a suction, like when drinking from a straw. Picture me drinking water from a glass at a restaurant while plugging my nose just as the waitress passes by with a slightly horrified look. It has happened. I tried not to laugh at their reaction because when I laugh with liquid in my mouth, it always shoots out of my nostrils. On the upside, I have a built-in nasal rinse system!

- **I now drool**. The combination of having no lower teeth to back up my recessed and deformed lower lip has left me with the inability to stop fluids from pooling up and draining onto my chin. Not as sexy as it sounds.

- I get waves of **face-contorting spasms** daily. I've had random spasms in my jaw muscles (masseters) that are extremely painful. A recent series of Botox injections seems to have them temporarily in submission.

- **I struggle to keep my weight up** to 155 lbs on an all-liquid diet. I was 240 lbs in the year of my original diagnosis. After my first round of chemo and radiation in 2013, I was able to maintain a weight of 170 lbs, but now, on an all-liquid diet, I struggle to get up to 155 lbs.

Adjusting to the physical changes from my surgeries was challenging, but the practical realities of daily life brought struggles of their own. One of the most significant was learning to navigate the simple yet essential act of 'eating'—a process that would mold and reshape my relationship with food.

## Feeding Time

I am saddened about losing my ability to eat. You probably don't think about it, but nearly every business has food for sale, including drug stores, gas stations, and even Marshall's clothing stores. Ace Hardware in my town makes shoppers walk through a cash register 'funnel' lined with snacks to tempt their patrons while they wait their turn in line. Every commercial break on TV channels seems to advertise food and beverages. The worst? Walking through a supermarket. Utter torture. Food is everywhere, and every time I see it, I'm reminded that my eating days are past me.

Growing up, my father always said, "Eat to live. Don't live to eat." His advice years ago feels fresh and current to me now. Nonetheless, I miss

I don't get asked to join others for lunch or dinner anymore. I think the idea of eating in front of me—knowing I can't enjoy the food—makes people feel awkward or, worse yet, guilty.

It might sound a bit masochistic, but I still love cooking and baking, even though I can't taste the results when I do. Art relaxes my mind, whether with paint, a camera lens[9], or crafting an artisan-quality loaf of sourdough bread. You can watch me making my sourdough video before losing my entire tongue on YouTube at https://tinyurl.com/5n8cj329.

Embracing my new reality has been more difficult than I expected. Of course, I didn't know what to expect, but my days have, at times, been overwhelming. There are so many things to do that I never had to think about prior to the day I lost my tongue—especially related to "eating."

When I returned from the hospital, I tried eating some chocolate pudding. It turns out our tongues not only help guide food towards our molars for chewing, but they also act as a conveyor belt of sorts, moving food backward so we can swallow it. When I closed my mouth on the pudding, I could actually taste it some—which seemed like a miracle without tastebuds—but it just sat there and didn't move. Next up was trying to eat some chocolate chip mint ice cream. Not only could I not chew the chocolate bits because I have no lower teeth, but the melted ice cream drained more into my sinuses and out my nose than it did down my throat. On the upside, the taste buds on the roof of my mouth can taste bitter, so the only 'food' I consume orally is beer, which I can drink at the rate of about 4oz an hour.

---

[9] https://roberthaase.myportfolio.com/photography

Food and shared meals are at the core of our social culture. Eating together is the grout of conversation, filling the voids between thoughts to help minimize uncomfortableness. Even toying with our food with a fork can be a reason to divert our gaze.

At first glance, a section of my kitchen counter looks like a science lab. A pill sorter box with the 32 pills and capsules of medicines and supplements I take every day, a glucose monitoring kit to track my body's reaction to my formula throughout the day, a canister of blended probiotic protein powders, a Cuisinart hand stick blender, a 'Silent Knight' pill crusher, a mortar and pestle for me to pulverize the chunks of pills into a fine powder, two three-sided mixing/pouring containers, cartons of my flavorless adult meal replacement formula. Every night at about 8:00 pm, I mix my formula, protein powder, pulverized pills, and supplements, pour the mixture into a large Mason jar, and let it sit overnight for my morning feedings. I'll also brew a pot of strong coffee and let it cool in the refrigerator overnight to help thin the mix for breakfast. Next, I do the same for my final evening feeding. I use a couple of oversized syringes to get the liquid nutrition into my stomach through my PEG[10] tube (Percutaneous Endoscopic Gastrostomy tube) for my five daily feedings. When I'm at home, I can sit on a chair in my kitchen, pull up my

---

[10]  https://my.clevelandclinic.org/health/treatments/4911-percutaneous-endoscopic-gastrostomy-peg

shirt to access my PEG tube, flush the line with cold water, and then use a syringe body as a funnel to begin getting the 20oz of formula mixture into my belly, 2oz at a time.

Each day's preparation process is a lot of work and doesn't bring with it the 'joy of cooking' that I used to have, making myself eggs and steel-cut oats for breakfast or flipping a steak on a backyard barbeque, although preparing meals for my parents helps fill the void somewhat. Don't get me wrong. I love to cook, but mixing the ingredients with a Cuisinart stick blender doesn't satiate the desire for meal preparation. The time-consuming tasks for meal prep at home are far less convenient in the front seat of my car while on the road, at a hotel, or worse yet, on a packed airplane during long flights.

For a recent six-hour flight to Hawaii, I packed cartons of formula and a reusable Bolee Bag[11] system into my carry-on luggage. As I sent it on the TSA conveyor/scanner, I left a signed doctor's note explaining my medical need for nutrition through an abdominal tube. I was a little uneasy because I could only communicate by writing on my writing tablet. I felt like a terrorist about to hand the agent a note. Not suspicious at all, right?

As expected, the scanner agent pulled my bag aside, flagging it for manual inspection. The letter fell to the side as the agent pulled the one-gallon Ziplock bag with

---

[11] https://www.udelivermedical.com/store/Bolee-Bag-p229624475

liquid formula cartons out of the carry-on bag. She looked across the conveyor belt at me with a suspicious 'stink-eye' as I held up my writing board with one hand spelling out in all caps: "LOOK AT THE LETTER!" Meanwhile, I pointed towards the letter that had fallen aside with my other. She gave me a confused look, so to save time while exposing myself to public embarrassment, I lifted my shirt to reveal the PEG tube. Do you know how sometimes guys in movies or commercials lift up their shirts to show off their '6-pack abs' or to show they are packing a firearm? Yeah, that wasn't me. She saw the 8.5" tube that was penetrating my abdomen. Her eyes got big. I flipped my board over to show the sticker that read, "I can hear you, but I am unable to speak." After reading it, she somehow thought that talking loudly while exaggerating her lip movements would help me hear what she was going to do next. Sigh.

The whole screening process was a bit embarrassing because all the bags pulled for inspection were piling up behind mine. One glance over my shoulder revealed several travelers looking at their watches with folded arms while breathing in exaggerated huffs as if making their agitation known to me would magically speed things up.

After the TSA agent swabbed my canisters, bag, and palms for explosives, I repacked my bag and made my way to the gate.

Three hours into my flight, I could feel my stomach rumbling. I needed to feed myself. I pulled the Bolee Bag from my carry-on, poured in a canister of formula, added water, and then pulled my PEG tube out between the buttons in my shirt. It helped that I planned for this rather than wearing a pullover shirt or sweater. I did my best to be discreet, as most people had never seen such an oddity.

Rather than allow the fluid to drain by gravity like usual, I squeezed the bag to speed up the process. After flushing the PEG tube with water, I tucked it away for later and went back to reading my book. Even though the five-minute process was hidden from most of the other passengers, it still felt a little humiliating. It's not the same as breastfeeding, but to feed, I have to make myself vulnerable and expose a part of myself that is personal. Moments later, the Alaska Airlines flight attendant came by, handing out those incredible Biscoff Cookies. I used to love eating those cookies. The truth is, I miss food. A lot.

There are days when I feel like I should be in one of those old circus side shows, side by side with Tom Thumb, the world's smallest man, the "bearded lady," and the Siamese twins, Chang and Eng. It has been over a year since I've lost my tongue, and to this day, all of my food goes through a freakish-looking tube into my belly. I have to sleep upright with seven pillows to prop me up in my bed. The best part is that I have a "gooey gunk" issue in that I don't produce normal saliva but a thick pinkish mucous. When it gets to the point that it starts blocking my airway, I have to toss back warm water and cough it out into the sink. Well, that's how it used to work. Now, all of my throat 'goo' passes through my right sinus and nostril, forcing me to close the other nostril with my finger and blow out the glob with a quick exhalation. Maybe it's a cross between a party trick and a sideshow freak, but either way, it isn't something that lends itself well to working in a business or government setting. I fear that this issue might continue to degrade, which could easily be an excuse for elective agoraphobia.

I'm impressed at how accommodating my friends and family have been to my repulsive side effects. It's gross. Some days, I feel like a scene in the space parody movie *Galaxy Quest*, when the Thermians transport one of their own into a gooey mess when it arrives inside out[12]. Those who haven't watched Galaxy Quest are missing out on some great comedic therapy.

Adjusting to new ways of eating was a challenge, but the harder part was facing the emotional toll of every-

---

[12] https://youtu.be/IipR1LUYRZI

thing I had been through—a darkness I couldn't ignore any longer.

## Facing the Darkness

Rather than 'bury the headline,' I'll say it and get it out of the way: Yes, thoughts of suicide have crossed my mind more than once over the past year. My friends and family had no idea until they read this chapter. I didn't plan it or intend to hurt myself. I didn't exhibit any 'tale-tell' signs but thought about it.

I had experienced 'compound adversities' when I lost my wife, my home, my business, and my car. It happened again when later diagnosed with cancer, and years later, when I lost my entire tongue and then my job. Experiencing wave after wave of adversity barely allowed me to get a footing before being knocked over again.

It felt like torture or an emotional 'waterboarding' of sorts. Worse yet, these incessant instances of adversity led to compounded physical and emotional stress, mucking up my healing process. News of losing my tongue and losing my job felt like a combination of waterboarding while being knocked off of my feet before having a chance to stand. It was overwhelming. In truth, it was terrifying. With each pounding knocking me off my feet, I struggled to right myself again. I felt like the inflatable toy I had as a boy. I could punch it hard enough to lay it parallel to the floor, but it would pop back up each time. Each new adversity felt like another punch, but I knew I could recover.

Through it all, I've been blessed, but when I lost my tongue, my world was rocked. I could never have imagined not being able to pick up the phone to call a friend or call a business when I might have a question. Realizing I can't speak is scary, and knowing I can never again say, "I love you" is depressingly sad.

As someone who encourages others and tries to inspire with hope, reading that I've considered suicide probably sounds a little 'off-brand.' What's even more unsettling is that after working for a couple-year stint at the Thurston County Coroner, assisting in autopsies, I had the chance to read several reference books on the subject of suicide and other ways to die. I know many ways of doing it successfully without leaving behind a mess for whoever found my body. In the end, dying is easy. Living is hard.

Why am I admitting to this? Why reveal my weaknesses in writing? If my story can encourage others, they need to know I'm not superhuman or unusually tenacious in my zest for life. Thoughts of suicide are common when people lose what's most important to them or when life seems impossible because of 'dire' circumstances.

Suicide and death are subjects most people don't want to think about. Publicly, I've heard people say, "I would never..." when it comes to ending their own lives. I know I've said it. Proudly, even before the first time, I considered it.

While death is usually random, like a mortal game of musical chairs, suicide is a choice. When the ache, sadness, or hopelessness becomes too much, suicide can be the ultimate pressure relief valve—a way out of current circumstances. 'Current' is the key word here because heartache and hopelessness are transient states of emotion. Looking for a permanent solution to a temporary problem isn't logical.

I have always been a logical thinker. Although my actions have often defied logic, I lean on logic for most decisions. When it comes to thoughts of suicide, rational thinking is a life-saver.

According to some studies, drugs and alcohol are involved in as many as half of all suicides[13]. That's a lot.

I remember the first time I ever considered suicide. It was when my girls' mother and I were in the early stages of the divorce process. Divorce can be ugly enough on its own, but add in the potential of 'losing' your children, and you have the makings of immeasurable anguish. I

---

[13] https://mentalhealthcommission.ca/what-we-do/suicide-prevention

tried getting drunk to take away the heartache, but it only served to exacerbate my dark thoughts. Sober, I reflected on a list of 'Pros' and 'Cons' of ending my life. Addressing this with a simple list of reasons I should or shouldn't might sound silly. I wasn't thinking about being dead, just no longer *being*. As in Shakespeare's Hamlet, "To be, or not to be…" I wondered if it would be better for me simply 'not to be.'

As I struggled to find a reason to be—to continue—I started creating a mental tally sheet of pros and cons. On the pro side, my heartache would go away; my girls wouldn't feel torn between two parents whose marriage was falling apart; my wife would be free to marry a better man, and my life insurance would pay off the mortgage while providing funds for my three daughters' education.

Writing a list of cons while in 'the pit of despair[14]' took longer, but I stuck with it. Ultimately, the list was more prolonged. My reasons not to commit suicide came down to these:

- I would be missed by those I loved and loved me.

- I would inflict life-long emotional wounds on my daughters.

- I would miss out on raising my girls, even if it was for a few hours a month.

---

[14] The Princess Pride, directed by Rob Reiner (1987), 20th Century Fox

- It would send my girls the message that murdering myself was a viable option by setting such a horrific example.

After reading through the pros and cons, I heard a still, small voice saying, "Bob, a year ago, you would have thought that the very idea of ending your life was crazy." As I sat in the corner of my bedroom, I had to purge all of the negative thoughts, which began with an 'ugly cry.' The kind that is filled with heaving sobs that left me hoarse and with eyes so swollen that it's hard to see.

As I tried to make sense of it all, my thoughts wafted back to the Christmas movie *It's a Wonderful Life*, where Clarence, the angel, shows up on the bridge. The lead character, George, is about to jump from a bridge until Clarence shows him what his town and life would have looked like if it hadn't been for all the good he had done.

At that point, I needed to start listing all of the blessings in my life. My list was simple at first:

- I had a warm place to sleep and a roof to keep me out of the rain.

- I had food in my stomach.

- I had friends and family that loved me and daughters that adored me.

- I helped others in my profession.

- I didn't live in a war zone.

- I wasn't being persecuted for my religious beliefs.

Each day, I thought of new blessings to be thankful for. The process of looking for even the smallest of blessings in our lives can be cathartic and a 'vaccine' of sorts from allowing thoughts of suicide to gain the upper hand. I know the process was for me. I knew why I shouldn't contemplate thoughts of ending my life, but that doesn't mean those thoughts won't or haven't crossed my mind when I wasn't expecting them.

Even now, as I approach retirement age, I am worried about what lies ahead. The Great Recession and my bouts of cancer wiped me out financially, and I don't have the means to retire. I also don't want to be a burden on my daughters. Thoughts of ending my life still creep in with the belief that doing so would be a relief valve and solve my concerns.

Every day is a fresh opportunity to approach life by choice. Some people struggle with the idea of 'checking out' of life more than others, and while I've been successful at keeping negative thoughts under control, others experience the temptation much more.

That difficult process taught me that if I needed encouragement, I should start by encouraging others. That thought might sound counterintuitive, but it's not. In our society, I regularly see memes and hear messages that we should all look out for 'number one' and put ourselves first. While self-care is one thing, siloing off my energy serves just one person. However, if everyone cared for and blessed others, everyone would get blessed and have others watching out for them by having their backs.

Being empathetic, listening without judgment, and showing concern can save a life. For me, messaging friends helped me reconnect and get my mind in a better place. It wasn't that I needed to hear their sage wisdom, but have someone patient enough to hear about my worries and fears.

Asking for help doesn't equate to weakness. It takes courage to admit being at the bottom of an emotional pit and not seeing a way out.

Just because most people exhibit clues pointing to their decision to end their lives doesn't mean everyone does. Earlier this year, I had a friend surprise everyone when he killed himself. I had known him for over 30 years. He was always a vibrant, positive, and encouraging man. He was larger than life, athletic, healthy, charismatic, and engaging until he was gone—in an instant. Nobody saw a sign, not even me. Just writing this makes my heart sink, saddened at the thought of living without his positive presence in this world.

After hearing from my mother and Sara, Holly's reflections provided another layer of understanding, showing how my journey had touched her life in unique and meaningful ways.

## Holly's Reflection on My Adversity

Holly, my youngest daughter, lived with me full-time back in the fall of 2013 when I was going through chemotherapy and radiation therapy. There was no hiding the side effects of my treatments or when I would fall apart emotionally when I was having a hard time enduring the nausea and fatigue. Even though Ashley and Sara shared in shouldering responsibilities during my treatment, Holly was one of the ones who observed my process the most, 24 hours a day during that time.

I mentioned earlier that each of my girls has uniquely different personalities. Holly, my youngest, is my 'empath,' and like me, she viscerally feels the pain and emotion of others. While that gift can be helpful when trying to support a friend who is having difficulty articulating their feelings, it can be hell when helping a parent who has been battling cancer for over 16 years.

Because of her unique perspective on my journey, I asked Holly to share her thoughts, observations, and feelings from her years supporting me when I needed it most.

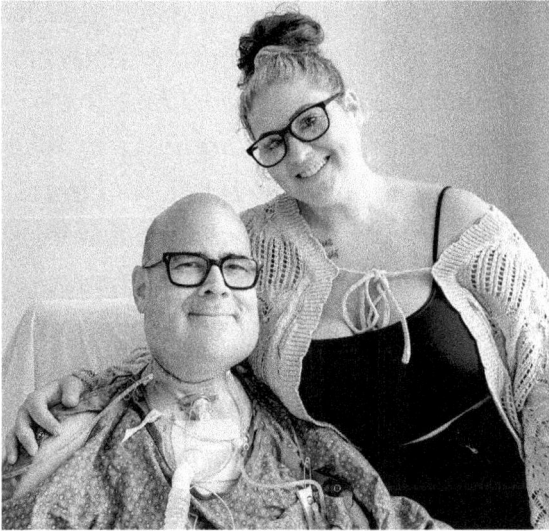

Holly with me in the hospital.

From Holly:

*Growing up with parents that I loved deeply, I always had an unwavering belief that they were invincible. They were always right and the image of perfection. But as I got older, I realized they were simply human. Like everyone else, they are flawed individuals who experience pain, regret, and hurt.*

*It can be quite a rude awakening. For me, that awakening came sooner rather than later when my parents decided to divorce. I was the youngest of three daughters, and I had little understanding of what was happening and, more importantly, why it was happening.*

*I would lose sleep over the safety and well-being of my parents. When I was at Dad's house, I was convinced someone would break into my Mom's house and attack and hurt her. When I was at my Mom's and my Dad would travel for work, I was convinced something would happen at the airport or that his plane would crash.*

*In both instances, I believed it was my responsibility to be there and save them from these disastrous scenarios. The potential catastrophes I was able to concoct in my overly active imagination were seemingly endless.*

*Enter, 2008.*

*My middle sister, Sara, was my pillar of support. She protected me from an abusive stepparent, looked out for me, and always reminded me that I wasn't a bad person. Her departure as an exchange student to another country was a significant loss, but her love and support remained with me.*

*I was in so much distress that my non-animal-loving mother got me a dog to cope with the sorrow of Sara not being around.*

*And then? My Dad was diagnosed with cancer.*

*It was overwhelming and simultaneously underwhelming, and nothing like what I'd seen in TV shows or movies. No chemo or radiation were needed. Every so often, Dad's doctor would find new cancer cells, remove them, and he'd be declared to be cancer-free once again.*

*It was heavy and scary but manageable. Of course, the doubts were constantly present, but it was as if the prior years of constant fear and worry had somewhat numbed the intensity of it all.*

*With my sister's return and the start of high school, it felt like we were finally getting back to normal. The routine and familiarity of everyday life brought a sense of relief and hope for the future.*

*I wouldn't say I thrived in high school; I was a neurodivergent gal who grew up being bullied and was familiar with not fitting in. On top of that, I was battling my own health issues that led to me missing out on chunks of school due to doctors' appointments, procedures, and surgeries. I was losing interest in my hobbies and my passions and had a hard time with my mental health in addition to the physical.*

*With my Dad's health complications, I felt a sense of guilt for having health problems of my own. I was experiencing intense chronic pain, a health issue that was time-consuming for my parents and no doubt difficult for them to witness. The added stress of my father's worsening health took a toll on my mental health, exacerbating my symptoms and making it even more challenging to cope.*

*But, I made it through high school, enjoying the fact that I was a senior and so close to leaving the town that never felt important or safe to me.*

*And then Dad's doctor found the tumor. It was the year I graduated high school, and Dad's cancer began to worsen. I don't think anyone in my family anticipated how different it would be this time—no little chunk of cancer, no minor surgery to remove it, and no quick remission.*

*This time, we all broke—at least a little. For me, that included seeing my Dad in and out of consciousness at a hospital in Mexico on my graduation trip; messaging my college professor to request an extension on an assignment because I was in the hospital with my Dad after he fell on the stairs and struck his head; seeing him in a coma following chemotherapy; hearing his doctors tell us he'd likely have brain damage after he'd collapsed while home alone, due to lack of oxygen, pneumonia, systemic sepsis, and respiratory failure; hearing the words "If he wakes up..." come out of the doctor's mouth; and needing to sleep on a cot in his room to make sure he didn't stop breathing in the middle of the night. It was so overwhelming for me.*

*As a girl with a bad case of OCD, it all felt like confirmation that every fear I had ever concocted was valid.*

*The five stages of grief are pretty universal. My Dad's battle with cancer showed me that the grief in my life would always be met with a 6th stage: guilt. Guilt that I hadn't done enough for my Dad. Guilt that I had my own traumas that, at times, took precedence over being present with him. Guilt that I hadn't been a perfect daughter. Guilt that I had no clue how to navigate everything else alongside all of the grief.*

*For some time after Dad went into remission, I operated from a place of fear, doubt, and shame. Everything felt heavy. It was beyond challenging to navigate adulthood, mental illness, and physical pain while also seeking healing and safety within my own self-discovery.*

*It's not fair. It wasn't fair then, and it's not fair now. Dad had already been through this. He's already stared down an early death far too many times, always coming out the other side. He shouldn't have to do it again because it's not fair.*

*But cancer doesn't care.*

*The cancer's return hasn't been made any easier by the fact that we've been here before. I can honestly say it's been so much heavier this time around. Cancer is aggressive and unpredictable, and at times, I feel as terrified and alone as I was in my adolescence. But the girl I was 10 years ago is not the woman I am today.*

*I've had 10 years of life experiences, self-discovery and education, healing, and therapy. Ten years of family get-togethers, being my Dad's favorite hugger, and rolling my eyes at his silly Dad jokes.*

*I've learned in this life that healing is not linear. The return of my Dad's cancer brought back a lot of aches and pains that I thought I had let go of. No one lives forever, and with age comes the clarity that although this grief is immense, so is the joy.*

*So yes, it's not fair. It's gut-wrenching, and it's soul-crushing, and sometimes, I genuinely have no clue how to navigate everything else alongside all of the grief again.*

*But no matter what has come before or what comes next, there's been so much joy.*

*The joy of hearing my Dad laugh again. The joy of seeing where I get so much of my resilience from. The joy of my Dad being alive to meet his grandson. The joy that medicine and science continue to give us more time.*

*Nothing is permanent, and no one lives forever. There is so much joy in the grief, and I will continue to cherish all of it.*

Holly's words reminded me of the deep connections formed through shared struggles. They also made me reflect on how pain, while difficult, could lead to a greater sense of purpose and meaning in life.

## Pain and Purpose

Focusing on our physical and mental anguish intensifies our pain. In my seminars, I reinforced the concept that a therapist's purpose is not to treat pain but to treat unhealthy tissue. If pain were all that mattered, we would ignore the person with quadriplegia who uses a wheelchair and is bleeding from a leg and yet doesn't feel a thing. Pain is nothing more than an indicator that something isn't right. The sensations from the pain itself will always be in flux.

People's pain thresholds are organically elastic, affecting how much they can handle. It's more of a changing barometer than a consistent level. Much like a woman who has begun her labor contractions, each level of pain she reaches resets what she had previously believed to be the most she could tolerate. Like pain, how stress impacts us fluctuates as we move through life.

Some years ago, while I was clearing some blackberry vines in my front yard, I had a visit from my friend Gary. I was covered in dirt and garden debris and thoroughly soaked from the sweat dripping down my face. "Dude,"

Gary said, looking at my left arm. "You cut yourself. You're bleeding." I glanced down at my arm, and sure enough, there was a long scratch running from my wrist to my elbow, and the dried blood surrounding it told me it had been there for a while. Suddenly, I began to feel the pain from the blackberry thorns—pain that I had not felt until that moment. My mind had been busy. I had been feeling the sun on my face and the strain of my muscles working. I was enjoying the music blasting from my portable speaker. I had not felt that nine-inch gash on my forearm. Why? Because other sensory inputs kept my brain busy, drawing attention away from my arm.

In injury treatment, we refer to this phenomenon as the Gate Theory, or the Gate Control Theory, because of the invisible 'gates' that keep the pain out when you're distracted with other things. How does this apply to adversity? When we stop focusing on the obvious negative impacts of our current experiences and instead focus on what's good, what's important, and all the small blessings, whatever they are, the negatives pale and blend into the background.

Distraction can be the best type of relief for mental and physical pain. Not to say it's not important to get our emotions and body healthy, but relief from the repeated crashing waves of adversity can come by distracting ourselves from focusing on the source of our pain.

If you held your mobile phone horizontally at the bridge of your nose, blocking 90% of your view, all you would see was your phone. But if you push the phone further from your face, the phone gets smaller, and the world around you comes into view. If the phone represents your adversity, it is easy to see how pushing it away from your face can give you a better perspective on life.

In the years before I opened my hospital-based medical myotherapy school, I worked on-call for the Thurston County Coroner as an autopsy assistant. I had dissected cadavers in my anatomy training years before, but a corpse, drained of its natural fluids, is a lot like comparing beef jerky to a raw steak. Our muscles don't look like jerky. Autopsies gave me a real-life perspective of the human body, and my experience working with the deceased made it clear to me that our bodies are nothing more than living puppets tasked with carrying our spirits and consciences around. Our bodies start failing cell-by-cell, day in and day out. Parts will fail, and parts will be lost. If I can stop worrying about living forever and come to terms with my mortality, I can work to put my mind at ease. This knowledge alone has been instrumental to my ability to maintain a positive attitude amid the chaos of adversity.

In observing others and hearing stories of longevity, I've seen those with something to look forward to often defy the odds of dying earlier rather than later. From people dying in a hospital bed, holding on until the last member of the family can arrive to say goodbye, to a goal of living until they reach the 100-year milestone, having something to look forward to is its own type of medicine.

I was in a family waiting area of a hospital a few years ago and struck up a conversation with a man whose father's health was declining without an apparent reason as to why. The man could only postulate that his dad had no reason to live. Just saying those words choked the man up as he considered what he was saying. I asked him what his dad's favorite thing to do was, and he said, "Fishing. He loved to fish." I suggested he make reservations for a fishing trip when he gets home. Secure the boat and lodging, print out a photo of the travel documents and a picture of the lodge, and put them on his father's refrigerator. "Talk to him about the trip with excitement and hope, and in the week before you depart, arrange your next excursion. Tell him all about it when you get back home."

The 'magic sauce' of having hope and a plan for the future can help encourage patients to take their medications, get rest, and make better health choices as they look forward to the planned event. Hope for the future is a powerful thing.

Reflecting on how pain had shaped my purpose opened my eyes to something even more profound— gratitude's quiet but powerful presence. Even in the hardest moments, there were so many reasons to be thankful, and those became the foundation for finding joy amidst the struggle.

# Gratefulness

Experiencing loss came with a plethora of emotions, with my thoughts directing those emotions.

There are days I wake up and go on about my day alone and in places where I interact with others. By the time I get home at the end of the day, I feel like I am one of those often irritating mimes who do not speak yet talk with their exaggerated expressions and hand movements to mimic what they are trying to say. I haven't even started learning sign language (ASL) because no one in my family or circle of friends speaks it. I lean on writing and other nonsensical forms of speaking, often with my arms flailing, hoping my grunts and motions make sense, but they don't. I feel like a mime without makeup.

Living life without the ability to speak is hard. Even holding up my writing board to a stranger means I am counting on them to be able to speak English *and* decipher my handwriting without a decoder ring.

Sometimes, those "hard" experiences can morph into shame.

Before I lost my job, I had been prepping video camera equipment at the office to drive up to Bellevue, Washington, the following day. I thought through every aspect of what I would be doing and how my boss and the team would navigate the planned events. My eyes worked their way down the schedule of events and stopped when they came to the "working lunch." A local caterer was to bring in a variety of boxed lunches and an assortment of beverages. I stopped reading and looked up, trying to solve the problem of feeding myself while everyone else munched away at their stuffed hoagie and freshly baked cookies and washed them down with a soda. At my regular weekly meeting with my boss, I asked her if there would possibly be a room where I could go to feed myself in private. Her answer? "Do your feeding in the men's bathroom." Forget about the millions of airborne bacteria and filthy counters; this felt the same as being ostracized because of my abdominal tube. I might as well have gone out in the back alley by the garbage bins and shopping carts full of homeless possessions.

My boss's response made me feel shameful, as though my medical necessity was a burden and 'undue hardship' on the organization. Maybe this is a bit like how breastfeeding mothers felt before laws were put in place to safeguard them from being charged for public indecency. New York was the first state to decriminalize breastfeeding a child in public, and that wasn't until

1984[15]. I realize that whipping out my abdominal tube and feeding apparatuses doesn't equate to breastfeeding, but not being shown compassion and grace in my new physiological state made me feel like doing so would have been indecent exposure.

Dealing with the physical side effects of losing my tongue and the troubling hardships that came with it has been a challenge for me, and focusing on them only served to add to my emotional distress. It was when I looked beyond what was 'unfair' in all that I was experiencing that I could find reasons to be grateful. Having a job was clearly one of them, and in the big picture, I was grateful to have health insurance and an income to pay for all of life's expenses. I could have spent the time justifying my right to righteous indignation, but focusing on what I had to be grateful for was a better use of my time.

The summer after I had the first half of my tongue removed, my surgeon had suffered terrible burns on his hands due to an explosive gasoline fire. Surgeons need the use of their hands and his struggles during recovery were significant. Several years later, I interviewed him to discuss his experience with adversity, how it affected him, and his observations of how it affected his patients over the years.

---

[15] https://pmc.ncbi.nlm.nih.gov/articles/PMC6860490/

I asked the surgeon if he had observed any common traits among his patients who successfully navigated through adversity. "The patients I see who are successful in their journey come out with a clear sense of gratitude and humility," he said. "They don't tend to dwell on what they've lost but focus instead on what the experience has done for them. Believing in something that is greater and more important than yourself and recognizing that your life has meaning in its capacity to serve others—in whatever form or fashion—is the purpose of life. It is what's necessary to get through all of this.

Being grateful and present in the moment is a choice and a skill that can be developed with purposeful practice. One of the quotes that helped him was from the ancient Chinese philosopher Lao Tzu, which was, "If you are depressed, you are living in the past. If you are anxious, you are living in the future. If you are at peace, you are living in the present."

When I say that I lost 'everything' in my experiences with adversity, that's not really true compared to what others have experienced. In 1940, Dr. Viktor Frankl, a distinguished psychiatrist, became the director of the Neurological Department of the Rothschild Hospital, a clinic for Jewish patients. Although he obtained an immigration visa to emigrate to America, he never used it. Instead, he chose to remain behind and care for his aging parents.

The following year, Dr. Frankl married Tilly Grosser, a woman he met while living in Vienna. The two were among the last of the Viennese Jews the Nazis allowed to marry but were prohibited from bearing any children. When Tilly became pregnant a short time later, Nazis forced her to abort the baby[16].

In September of 1942, Dr. Viktor Frankl, his wife, and his elderly parents were arrested, herded into train cars, and taken to a Nazi concentration camp where they were immediately separated and stripped of everything they had in their possession, including a manuscript of a book Frankl had been writing. In four different concentration camps over three years, Frankl endured beatings, torture, starvation, sickness, hard labor, and inhumane treatment at the hands of the guards.

Despite the millions murdered in the Auschwitz concentration camp alone, Frankl was one of only 1,200 still alive when the Americans liberated the camp in 1945. After being set free, he learned that every one of his immediate family members had died at the hands of the Nazis except his sister, who had escaped to Australia before later being arrested.

No story about what I've lost could come close to those who endured the horrific, soulless actions of the Nazis. All I can share is what I've experienced, the pain of loss, and the eventual hope I have for the future.

---

[16] Viktor Frankl Institut. (2019). Viktor Emil Frankl. Retrieved December 17, 2019, from
https://www.viktorfrankl.org/biography.html

The year after Dr. Frankl was liberated, he systematically reconstructed his book manuscript, eventually publishing *Man's Search for Meaning*[17]. The book's central theme is that a person can lose everything except for how they choose to respond. While Dr. Frankl could not control the variables of his adversity, he could control his choices and how he responded to adversity. He lost everything and everyone he held dear before he wrote, "...everything can be taken from a man but one thing: the last of the human freedoms—to choose one's attitude in any given set of circumstances." While Dr. Frankl could not control the variables of his adversity, he could control his choices in how he responded to adversity. Frankl truly 'lost everything,' and by comparison, I am blessed to have so much.

So many find their value and acceptance of others in their physical appearance or believe they demonstrate their intelligence when they speak. For me, the ravages of cancer treatment took both. Now, I have to parlay my skills and gifts into other, more creative ways.

Time shouldn't be spent focusing on what I cannot do anymore. Rather, it should be spent considering the new reality of what I *can* do and what blessings I have in my life—even the smallest of blessings.

---

[17] Frankl, V. E., (1959) Man's Search for Meaning, Boston, Massachusetts: Beacon Press

Gratitude didn't just help ground me, but it also motivated me to action. I missed the purpose that comes with putting in a hard day's work. Returning to work was not just a practical necessity—it was a manifestation of my commitment to rebuild and thrive, no matter what challenges would come with it.

# PART THREE

## LESSONS IN RESILIENCE

# My Return to Work

One month after my surgery, I returned as the association's Director of Communications. Sure, I couldn't speak, but I was getting the job done, writing the weekly newsletter and editing other projects about 80% of the day. I was producing graphic arts content or editing videos when I wasn't writing. I communicated by email and text, and in face-to-face meetings, I brought my electronic 'Jot' writing tablet[18] to write down my communications. The best thing about the tablet was I could respond in real-time. The downside was displaying my lousy handwriting and not having 'spellcheck' built into the pen.

Each day was an exercise in determination. I didn't want to get up, mix my formula and vitamins, pour it into my tube, and get to my desk across town. Every morning was another argument with myself, but my reasoning won. I didn't only have to get to my office and finish my work—I had to give it all I had. I was doing

---

[18] https://myboogieboard.com

well, but my body was still healing and still dealing with side effects and cellulitis infections. It turns out that fighting infections is physically taxing on the body and often causes severe drowsiness. Still fighting infections, that drowsiness caused me to fall asleep several times during company Zoom calls. Oops. There's nothing like nodding off on camera for everyone to see.

At the same time, I had been working 40 hours a week during my twice-a-day radiation treatments. I would arrive at work by 6:30 a.m., leave for treatment at 8:15 a.m., be back at my desk within the hour, work through my lunch, and then leave at 3:45 p.m. for the day's second treatment. I felt increasingly worse as the days went on.

In the days that followed my 'onscreen pseudo-narcoleptic episodes,' my boss called me into her office and said, "Bob, you are one of the strongest people I know. You've gone through so much, yet you're still here rather than taking time to heal." Per my boss's strong encouragement, I took three months of Paid Family & Medical Leave, a Washington State program my organization lobbied against.

For the next three months, I took time to heal. I went for walks, read, went to my hyperbaric treatments in Seattle, and relaxed as much as possible.

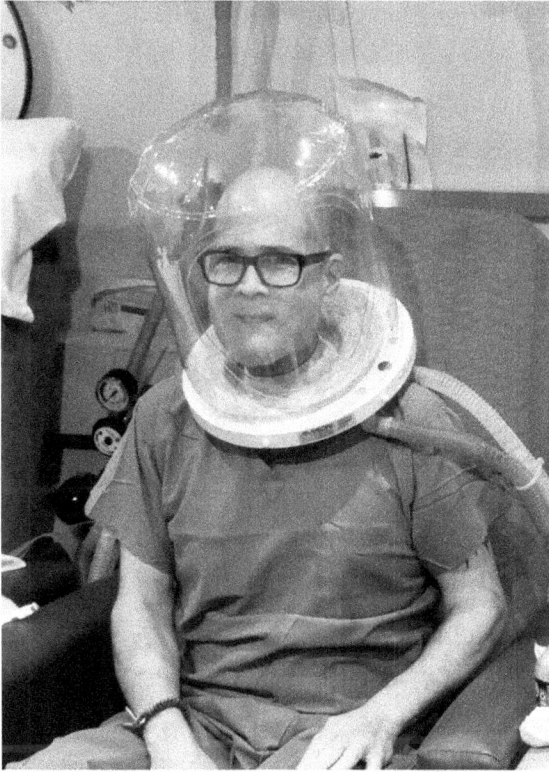

Wearing my bubble helmet during hyperbaric
treatments at Virginia Mason Hospital.

Taking time off from working wasn't easy for a guy
who's worked non-stop since the 6th grade. I wasn't
worried about returning to work because Washington
State requires employers to return employees to their
same—or nearly identical—job with the same duties,
responsibilities, status, pay, and benefits. My gut told me
that wouldn't be the case. I was rested and ready to
return to work after the three-month Paid Family &
Medical Leave period. Then, my boss informed me that

my position had been eliminated due to the organization's 'reorganization.' Turns out I was the only one reorganized out of a job.

I could see the irony in employing a communications director who couldn't speak, but sending me on my way was incongruent with their 'justice, diversity, equity, and inclusion' directives.

After three years of hard work, I walked away with three months of medical insurance. The experience left me feeling defeated, tossed aside, and worried. How was I going to afford over $1,350 a month in health insurance premiums? How would I pay my rent and my car expenses? The stress of it all was almost paralyzing at times.

My sudden job loss landed me on unemployment. I've never had trouble landing a job or finding clients for consulting work, but looking for communications-based work without the ability to speak has been more of a challenge. I can write, create graphics and web content, produce corporate videos, provide award-winning photography, and even write speeches. However, communicating on portable whiteboards, Boogie Boards, text, email, and chat apps isn't enough. My 'disability' is seen as a potential 'undue hardship' on potential employers.

I searched endlessly for agencies that support the 'mute' in our country, but there are none, at least none that go to the trouble of creating a website saying so. Are you blind? Check! Deaf? Check! In a wheelchair? It's not a problem. But if you cannot talk, good luck finding support from a government or non-profit organization.

Speaking of blind people (vision-impaired), I have to share one of my most embarrassing moments: Several years before my assistant, Charity, passed away, we were 'getting our steps in' by walking around downtown Des Moines, Iowa, and the district where we would present our seminar the next day. It was a sunny spring afternoon, and as usual, Charity and I were deep in conversation about whatever was on our minds.

Sign on post outside of the Iowa Department for the Blind.

Charity was like my sister, so we had regular arguments about life, philosophy, parenting, and current events. Walking back from downtown to our seminar venue, I saw a vision-impaired man with a tell-tale White Cane walking stick with a red-colored tip. Soon, I saw another and then another. Within minutes, I had seen over a dozen people walking around, tapping their walking sticks in front of themselves, navigating their way down sidewalks and across pedestrian walkways. I finally pointed the phenomenon out to Charity as we walked down the sidewalk and said, "That is so strange. I wonder why there are so many..." Just then, 'thwack!' I was interrupted as I walked my forehead right into a steel pole with a sign that read, *Iowa Department for the Blind.* Charity never let me live that down.

That memory was a slight detour on my way to saying that everyone has disabilities of some kind. Some are obvious, and some are hidden, but everyone has a different take on their challenges. Perspectives affect how people see themselves and assume how others see them.

It's curious how going month after month on unemployment and unable to find a job can undermine a person's self-worth, especially for those of us who tend to see our value in what we 'do' for a living. At least if I were an actor, I could say I was on 'hiatus,' but that excuse doesn't sound as believable for the rest of us. There are days when I've wondered if working a regular, 40-hour-a-week job would even be feasible given my new physical reality in the aftermath of treatment. The whole experience of looking for work came with challenges, but navigating the everyday moments—the routines and unexpected obstacles—truly defined my new reality. Living in this broken body is challenging, yet that's the hand I've been dealt. I can either play or fold.

Returning to work was a significant milestone for me, but it was Ashley's words that truly emphasized the resilience it took to get there. Her letter offered a heartfelt reflection on the strength she saw in me and the lessons she had learned throughout my journey.

## A Letter from Ashley

Many life-altering adversities affect more than a single person. They also affect our families, friends, and support networks. With this in mind, I asked my oldest daughter, Ashley, to share her experiences and observations of my cancer journey from her perspective. The following is what she wanted to share with my readers:

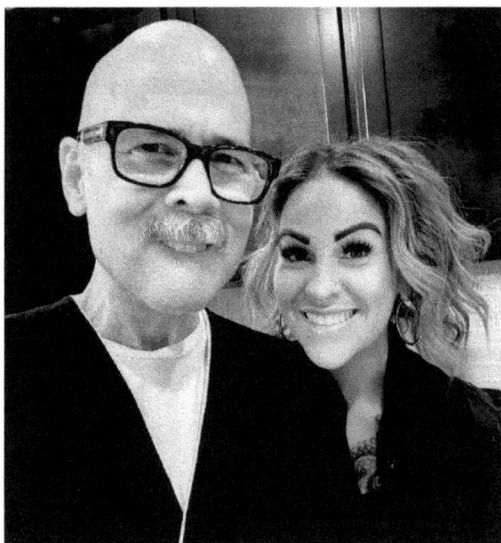

Ashley and me on Thanksgiving day, 2024.

From Ashley:

*Not to make this about me, but watching my Dad go through cancer has been the most challenging and heartbreaking experience of my life. When he was first seen by his doctors, they didn't label it "cancer," so it wasn't something I worried about. He just had "cells" on his tongue that his doctor would remove occasionally, and then he'd be good to go for a while. But it "wasn't cancer." When they finally put the cancer label on it, it was so scary for me. Everything was an unknown. Shortly before he was to have the first half of his tongue removed, I drove over to his house, and as soon as he opened the door, I just fell into his arms and cried. We had never been through anything like this before.*

*I was so mad at God. I didn't understand why this was happening. If he had been a smoker or chewed tobacco, then I wouldn't have been surprised if he ended up with tongue cancer. But my Dad didn't do either of those things. It wasn't fair.*

*At the time this was all happening, I had a job as a Community Service Officer that allowed me to use my sick time to help my Dad out with his medical appointments. I felt so blessed to be able to be in a position to do that for him. There were multiple occasions when I was at work when I shouldn't have been due to my mental state. Crying while you are driving someone to jail isn't a good look. I wish that I had known that I should have been more gentle with myself and taken the time off for my own care as well.*

*My recollection of my feelings and memories from the origins of my Dad's cancer story are a bit blurry in my mind, but I think that's because I want them to be. When pictures or updates 'memories' pop up of what I posted on Facebook from his diagnosis, through chemo, radiation, and the aftermath that followed, I skip past them. I try not to dwell on the details even though, deep down, I'll never forget them.*

*When I learned that my Dad's cancer had returned in 2023, it hit harder than the first time. Instead of unknowns, it brought back all of the pain, stress, anxiety, and horrible memories of what he had gone through the first time around. "Again!?" I thought. "Why do we have to do this again!?" Watching what he endured had been the worst time of my entire life, and now we had to do the same thing all over again. Talk about PTSD. He had already been through this, but this time, he would go through it with a body that was still weakened from the chemo and radiation, and he was a full decade older. Could his body even handle it again? What if it couldn't!?*

*I was able to drive my Dad to my sister's house the night before the surgery since she lived much closer to the hospital. We had a good night together. We ate dinner and sat in the hot tub, enjoying our time together. That night, my Dad took the time to record videos for us all. He wanted us to have videos of his voice in case that was the last time he could speak intelligibly. I made the mistake of watching the one he made for me and the one he made for my son before going to bed. I cried myself to sleep that night.*

*The next morning, we drove to the hospital, and when we walked into the surgery center, a wave of PTSD hit me. It looked exactly the same as it had ten years prior when we sat for hours during his first big surgery. I immediately started crying. It brought back everything. It was the last place we were with my Dad when he still had the voice I grew up with. It was the place where my grandpa passed out from a medical emergency while Dad was being prepped for surgery, and we mistakenly thought he had just passed away. I had never wanted to be in that place again, but there we were.*

*Once we got Dad checked in for surgery, we settled into a nook in the waiting room. The first time around, we had plenty of time to sit and talk together before he was taken back, and then we were allowed to go back one at a time to visit with him while they were getting him prepped. This time, though, a nurse came out to get him only minutes after we sat down and informed us that we wouldn't see him until after surgery. We couldn't go back to visit with him like before? I thought we had a few hours, at least, but no. It was time to say goodbye. No more time to process; no more time to sit together and mentally prepare. That moment was traumatizing. After Dad had been taken back, my sister and I just sat and cried. It was so abrupt and deeply upsetting. My youngest sister couldn't be there that day, so we FaceTimed her and filled her in on how traumatic the experience was.*

*Two weeks later, when my Dad was finally able to come home from the hospital, it was all hands on deck. We all took turns staying with him at his house, changing his wound dressings, making sure he got his medication and his liquid nutrition pumped into the tube hanging from his stomach on time, making sure that he didn't stop breathing while he was asleep. You might understand the feeling if you've ever had a newborn baby, a child of any age, or care for anyone's wellbeing. When each of us covered overnight shifts, we would wake up multiple times in the middle of the night just to listen to make sure he was still breathing.*

*Finally, after a few weeks, we 'let him' be on his own again. It was still stressful, though, especially considering that he literally almost died when he was on his own the first time around. But at some point, you just have to trust that he's not alone. God's got him.*

*During the summer of 2023, a few months before the cancer had returned, one of my coworkers randomly asked if we could go to church with her the next day. We had started going back to church a few years prior, but Covid had stopped that. My coworker had lost her father to cancer just a couple of years prior. She shared advice from what she learned when her Dad was going through his cancer and prayed for me. I am so grateful that God placed her in my life. I'm so thankful for the place I was at when this all happened again. This time, I had many compassionate co-workers and friends, many who shared my Christian faith.*

*This time around, many things were different. Ten years ago, my sisters were still young, so being the oldest, I was essentially in charge of things. This time around, I have a young son. My sisters have been able to step in more. One of them has essentially taken my place of being 'in charge,' and I couldn't be more grateful that she has.*

*I am so thankful to have my sisters. I do not know how I would have made it through all of this without them. I have times when I feel so guilty for only having one child. I start spiraling. What if I end up getting cancer one day, and my son has to go through the same things my sisters and I have had to go through, but he has to do it alone? That question haunts me.*

*When you watch someone so close to you go through cancer, it becomes a trigger word for sure. You become so sensitive to the topic. It's very hard watching a loved one go through cancer, and there is little you can do to make it better. You can't fix it or take away their pain. All you can do is be there for them. If anything, I feel guilty. Guilty that I'm healthy, guilty that I can taste food, guilty that I can speak clearly. In reality, I know it should only remind me to never take those things for granted.*

*I always have been and always will be worried about my Dad. From all of the things that happened over a decade ago, especially when he was found at the brink of death, to the struggles he faces today. So many things could happen, so many things could go wrong. The worst will always linger in the back of my mind. It will al-*

*ways be there, even if I try to push it back and bury it. My greatest fear is that because of everything he's been through, it will inevitably shorten his life. Whether his body just can't last as long as it would have if it hadn't gone through cancer and the subsequent treatments, or if one of the infections comes back and the doctors can't get it under control, or the cancer comes back again and they just can't fix it. That is my greatest fear. I worry that cancer will inevitably rob us of the time we have left with my Dad.*

*One thing I have learned this time is to compartmentalize. I noticed it started when I was pregnant, and my Dad had a different emergency medical event. I had to separate what was going on with my Dad from what was happening with me. It was probably only a month or so before my giving birth, so I could not allow my stress about my Dad's situation to overwhelm me. My compartmentalization continued with the return of his cancer. Sometimes, I feel guilty for being able to compartmentalize. I feel guilty for living my life while my Dad goes through all that he is going through. But then I have to remind myself that it won't do anybody any good if I remain in a constant state of worry. I have to be present for my family.*

*Watching my Dad fight cancer for the last six-teen years has shown me that attitude is every-thing. I fully believe that if my Dad had not had the positive outlook and attitude that he has, he would not still be here. Was it easy to stay posi-tive? I guarantee it was not, but he did it. I'm proud to be his daughter. I'm so proud of his beating the odds and how hard he has fought. Saying my Dad is strong and resilient is an un-derstatement.*

*When my Dad is no longer on this earth, it will be beyond devastating. However, I find comfort in knowing that he will have a new body in Heaven.. A new body that has never felt the pains of cancer, a new body that will allow him to have his once powerful 'radio' voice back, a new body that can smell and taste and eat all of the deli-cious foods that he can no longer eat in his cur-rent body. I find peace in knowing that he loves God and will be able to experience these things again one day.*

*I'm blessed not to have been alone ten years ago or last year when the cancer returned. My husband has always been there to support my extended family and me. He is always willing to help whenever anyone needs him. I am so thank-ful for him. I'm also thankful for my son. My Dad didn't have any sons, and my son is likely to be his only grandchild. Occasionally, when I look at my son, I can see a glimpse of my Dad. There is definitely a family resemblance. I find solace in the fact that even when my Dad isn't here anymore, in a way, I will still be able to see him.*

*A few things stuck out to me in one of my devotions recently. It said that without fear, we would never know faith, and without hurt, we would never know hope. It also said that some lessons can only be learned in the midst of chaos. Of course, I wish my Dad never had cancer or had to go through the things he's gone through, but I also know that, as the devotional said, without the hard times, we would not appreciate the good as much. The fear and the hurt that come with cancer can still be made good by allowing me to know the hope that can come from drawing deeper into my faith.*

*My Dad's cancer brought healing. That sounds a little backward, but it's true. His cancer brought healing in our family, but most importantly, between him and my mom. Like most divorces, theirs wasn't pretty or easy. After his first major surgery, my Dad, mom, and I met with a counselor at the place where he received his radiation. I honestly don't remember what we talked about during the counseling session, but I do remember the healing that seemed to take place surround-*

*ing the time of his surgery and treatments. My mom and my stepdad visited my Dad in the hospital, and they prayed for him, and they came to his house and helped him out. My parents were able to tell each other that they loved each other again. I can't speak to how they each experienced it from their perspectives, but as their daughter, it has been incredible to witness their relationship's healing and repair. Seeing how far they've come is so special and means so much to me.*

*I love the quote, "Don't tell God how big your storm is; tell your storm how big your God is." This can be hard to remember sometimes, especially in the midst of the storm. This time, I am in a much better place than I have ever been in my relationship with God, and I know for a fact that leaning on Him has been and will always be what gets me through any storm life throws my way.*

Ashley's words highlighted the strength we had built through adversity, reminding me that resilience isn't something we're simply born with—it's a skill that grows stronger each time we face and overcome challenges.

## Resilience is a Muscle

I didn't wake up one morning and find I was resilient. It was something I had to build, one setback and adverse event at a time, much like a muscle. While resilience can be taught by a parent's example or by taking a survivalist course, nothing builds resilience like enduring adversity. We either die from it, or we grow from it. As Friedrich Nietzsche said, "That which does not kill me makes me stronger[19]."

Every encounter with adversity forces change, for both good and bad. Just as a bad relationship might turn someone into a hermit, it could also lead them to personal growth, fortitude, and wisdom that will prepare them for their next exposure to adversity.

---

[19] Translated from German "Was mich nicht umbringt macht mich stärker." Nietzsche, Friedrich, Twilight of the Idols, or, How to Philosophize with a Hammer (German: Götzen-Dämmerung, oder, Wie man mit dem Hammer philosophiert) Published 1889.

Most people emerge from significant adversity as a changed person[20], or at least with an altered perception. Many say, "I just want to return to how things were before." The truth is that seldom happens. Life goes on, and adversity shuffles the deck, often making a return to normal impossible. That said, the very nature of life is all about change. We can't go back, but we can be thankful for what we have, not the least of which is that we are still alive.

Just as a blown-over tree will never return to how it was positioned before, it can adapt and grow upwards. Sure, it will look like the shape of an 'L,' but it will reach skyward in search of the sun. Different? Yes. But the tree can thrive again, as can we all.

Some define adversity as the experience or continued experience of difficulty, hardship, distress, or misfortune. Others say it involves facing significant challenges, obstacles, or problems that test a person's resilience and strength.

Adversity can take many forms: personal setbacks, loss, health issues, financial struggles, or being emotionally affected by the most recent political elections. Adversity allowed me to grow, forcing me to dig deeper, redefine my limits, and ultimately emerge stronger or wiser on the other side.

---

[20] Stephen Joseph, PhD, Lisa D. Butler, PhD (2010) Positive Changes Following Adversity. *PTSD Research Quarterly VOLUME 21/NO. 3 – SUMMER 2010*

For me, adversity brings depth to my perspective. In the 1975 movie *Monty Python and the Holy Grail*, there is a scene where two knights are sword fighting, and the better fighter cuts the arm off of his adversary, who says, "Tis but a scratch!" After he cuts off his second arm, the adversary says, "Just a flesh wound!" After his right leg gets cut off, he yells, "I'm invincible!" Finally, after losing both arms and legs, the adversary says, "We'll call it a draw." Absurd? Yes, but I think that movie prepared me for my attitude as I would continue facing the surgeons' scalpels hacking away at my body over time.

All of us experience adversity differently on our own bell curve. Someone who stubs their toe may experience an eight out of ten on their scale, but when a woman experiences her first labor pain, it will reset her pain threshold—as will the next. Regardless, what I perceive is usually what I receive. In other words, if I expect pain, pain is what I will get. Fear of what will come only breeds fear because expectations affect how experiences are interpreted.

In my medical myotherapy courses, I asked patients to rate their pain level on a one-to-ten scale at the start of each treatment and what they couldn't do because of the pain. I found that function always improved faster than their *perception* of pain and dysfunction.

Again, all adversity involves the lack of, or loss of, something or someone. It could be the loss of a limb or the ability to walk. In my case, I lost more than my tongue. At first, I lost the clear 'radio voice' I had honed and used in training videos, television and radio advertisements, and teaching seminars. Later, I lost my ability to speak at all. I also lost relationships, especially during my first rounds of chemotherapy and radiation treatments in late 2013. Some friends couldn't handle seeing the drastic changes to my face. I looked frail and nearly 100 lbs lighter. They stopped communicating and stopped coming by to see me. Meanwhile, others showed up, determined to bless me as best as they knew how.

Some losses are invisible. When a woman experiences the loss of her pregnancy to stillbirth, miscarriage, or even an abortion, most employers don't give time off as they would if an employee lost the baby after it emerged from her womb in a live birth. Why would they? From most employer's perspectives, it was 'just a fetus,' but to the expectant mother, it could have been the culmination of her life's dream to be a mother. When that woman is seen out in public, there are no signs of her loss. She doesn't wear an armband or other visible sign to represent the loss of her stillborn child. Her suffering continues in private, and her grief is processed in waves, often when it is least convenient.

The loss of a finger might be easier to process than the loss of a lifelong relationship, and both pale in comparison to the loss of a child. My losses don't compare to the loss of a life. I'm alive, and I am thankful for that every single day.

I never chose to experience the adversities I've had to face. These weren't experiences I wanted, but I've grown stronger because of them, not despite them. Life choices can offer something good in exchange for inevitable pain and loss in the future. If a person marries, for example, their marriage will end—either in divorce or in death. People take a chance on love and pray for the best, choosing joy, knowing it will eventually bring heartache and pain.

Life challenges will also test marriages and relationships. Couples who work to build a solid foundation before adversity strikes have a better chance of surviving and emerging stronger. The choice to stick with it and do the hard work can pay off. It's as though adversities experienced within a marriage are exercises, strengthening the bond and the relationship as the couple emerges from each experience.

The pain of hardship builds inner strength and emotional resiliency as each experience fortifies our resilience and strengthens our resolve. The more significant the difficulty, the more opportunity for change—potentially preparing us for our new life purpose.

**Reinforcement**

Since ancient times, masons have mixed horsehair into mortar and straw into bricks to help them maintain strength and durability under stress. After college, when I went to work for a pole-building company in Lynnwood, Washington. Doug, the assistant manager, wanted me to become familiar with the various features of the buildings they erected compared to the competition.

Over several days, we visited dozens of structures. Some were over a decade old, and some were newer. At each inspection, Doug pointed out the condition of the concrete slab floors and how they had held up over time. Oddly, some older buildings' concrete floors had no cracks, while some newer buildings had cracks throughout.

Doug explained the slabs that weren't cracked contained Fibermesh, which was a modern interpretation of the centuries-old techniques of adding horsehair and straw to mortar and concrete. The fibers, which look like short pieces of cut fishing line, are churned into the concrete during the mixing process.

The Fibermesh brochure showed before and after photos of three identical concrete blocks, each individually tested by the crushing force of a large hydraulic press. The first block was made entirely of concrete, the second had steel rebar reinforcement, and the third had Fibermesh blended in. The unreinforced concrete block crumbled under the pressure. The block with rebar cracked, but chunks of concrete broke away to expose the embedded steel bars, but the Fibermesh® block was mystifying. Rather than crumble, it uniformly held together while appearing almost malleable with limited distortion to its original shape, relying on the nearly invisible plastic fibers for strength. The difference in durability came from within.

Years later, I used those seemingly fragile plastic fibers in the foundation and floor of a concrete block building I built in the fall of 1999. Just over a year later, we were hit by the "Nisqually Earthquake" of 2001, which was 6.8 magnitude in scale. It was huge. While many buildings and roads throughout our region were found severely damaged after the shaking finally stopped, my concrete floor didn't have so much as a crack. The slab floor was strong — from within. The same is true for us.

Our capacity to avoid being crushed or destroyed by adversity comes from within us, and the combination of our thoughts, beliefs, faith, hopes, dreams, and desire to survive are components of our invisible reinforcement.

Strength comes from within. As adversity presses against us, our mind and body react, compensate, and provide an opportunity for the stress and pressures to strengthen us, which increases our resilience and produces what others see as courage. In the same way that your muscles are made stronger by stress and strain, your heart, mind, and resolve can also be strengthened.

Courage isn't just about strength alone; it's a component of strength, determination, perseverance, and perspective. Courage actively takes our thought processes captive, directing them by conscious choice.

Building physical and emotional resilience was essential, but I came to realize that true strength also required a deeper connection—a spiritual resilience to carry me through the challenges that lay ahead.

## Spiritual Resilience

I was raised in a church-going Christian home. In my youth, we went to Wednesday night, Sunday morning, and Sunday evening services. Church felt like a second home, especially our youth group, which was large and full of students from schools all over the county. At church, I learned the difference between being 'religious' and being a follower of Christ. I remember seeing a bumper sticker on a car in the church parking lot that read, "Christians aren't perfect, just forgiven." True. I can't be good enough to earn my way to heaven.

As an adult, I came to understand that my actions speak a lot louder than my words. Sure, I can argue the finer points of religion or discuss church dogma, but I would much rather exhibit my faith by loving, supporting, and encouraging others. The reality is, however, that society loves labels and tends to judge people based on one or two-word descriptors. I'd much rather be referred to as 'Christ-like' than a 'Christian,' mostly because people will judge others on that one word. That would be like a mass murderer identifying as a Democrat during a news interview and viewers deciding that all Democrats are bad because of the one bad seed.

All of that said, life, divorce, pandemics, financial crises, and other events can rock a person's faith. I know they have rocked mine. In the previous chapter, I discussed how people want to hold God accountable for everything that goes wrong but don't want to give up their free will. Those free will choices can be the originating catalyst for horrible things. In life, bad things happen, and 'nobody is getting out alive.'

One of the reasons I've done well in overcoming adversities is having perspective. One might think it was my attitude, but here is the truth:

**Attitude is what develops from perspective.**

The big picture is that I know I am going to die. I'm not fearful of dying, and that gives me a lot of freedom. It's also helped me build spiritual resilience. I know that my future is in God's hands regardless of the plans I make. When I pray, God will give me one of three answers: "Yes," "No," or "Not yet." I've learned that my timeframes are seldom His, and understanding that has helped me build patience. It has also given me freedom because my future is in His hands.

I didn't write this book to convince others to be Christians. Sure, I hope they consider Jesus' sacrifice for them on the cross, but it is important to know that salvation is a gift rather than something earned. I can never be good enough or do enough good things for others to earn my way into Heaven.

Throughout these 16 years of dealing with cancer, I've never seen myself as in a 'cancer battle.' A battle is something to be won or lost, and if I were to die, my family would say that I 'died of cancer' rather than I 'lost the battle.' I've made it for 16 years so far, which is longer than most people's experience with cancer. I also don't pray for healing or pray for the cancer not to come back. I've given this whole cancer thing to God and trust Him with my future. I pray for my life to matter, for me to be an encouragement to others, and for my life to make a difference in theirs. That prayer has yielded amazing results statistically, and I'll keep praying for the same.

### Would God give a person more than they can handle?

Here's a pop quiz for those who pray to God and look to the Bible for direction and comfort: True or False: "God will not give a person more than they can handle." The answer? False.

One of the most misquoted verses in the Bible isn't a verse at all. Nowhere does it say, "God will not give you more than you can handle." It's not true. If it were, what's the point in praying for help amid chaos and adversity if there was no need? In 1 Corinthians 10:13, the Bible says, He will not let a person be tempted beyond what they can bear. "But when you are tempted, he will also provide a way out so that you can endure it[21]." God *will* give a person more than they can handle—*on their own*.

While on the topic of God, I need to clarify that praying is important. Not because it is a guarantee that God will intervene and heal me physically but because praying can bring peace to my thoughts. Stress creates a chemical response, releasing stress hormones, which puts my body into a state that works against me—not for me. Prayer doesn't even have to be on my knees. I can leave my AirPods at home and go for a walk or trail hike. No music, just my thoughts. I've even kept a small notebook and a pen in my pocket to write down what comes to me as I've prayed and unwound. In modern times, I've not really seen many miracles, like an arm growing back or prayers raising people from the dead. Every faith healer that ever lived is either dead or will be by the time they reach 120 years of age or so. I believe the ultimate healing isn't in prolonging someone's life but when someone finds healing in their spirit and thoughts.

For those who aren't comfortable reaching out to God, my best suggestion is for them to reach out for support from friends, a sibling, other family members, or a professional therapist. Or, a combination of those

---

[21] 1 Corinthians 10:13 New International Version

who make up their 'tribe,' who they trust and always have their backs.

People need to be cautious when choosing their support people. A support person might very well know a situation well enough to give healthy advice, direction, or encouragement. On the other hand, some might receive unhealthy advice or be told what they want to hear rather than the hard truth. I've even known licensed mental health therapists and counselors who doled out dangerous suggestions. Everyone has an opinion, and the goal should be to find those who don't necessarily tell a person what they want to hear but help them see their situation from different perspectives and suggest safe actions that would lead to a positive outcome.

Choosing to confide in and seek counsel from the wrong people can send a person down a dangerous path. I was being sued some years ago, which could have destroyed my business and ruined me personally. I was in the right, but 'the court of public opinion' doesn't always care about the truth. I was visibly stressed, and it was affecting my health. As things were heating up, I was approached by someone who said she had a 'friend' who could take care of my problem. Puzzled, I thought, 'Wait... what?' and asked, "What do you mean?" She looked around to ensure she couldn't be overheard and whispered, "I have a guy that can make (the person suing me) permanently disappear." I didn't know the woman well. I knew she hung around with *unsavory* friends and believed her offer to be legitimate. I tell you this to say that when things are at their worst, people are more susceptible to bad advice. If I had taken her up on her offer of 'eliminating' my trouble, I would probably have written this book with a crayon from my private cell at the nearest federal prison.

Developing spiritual resilience taught me the importance of relying on the right resources and strategies. These tools became essential in navigating the ongoing challenges of my journey.

# PART FOUR

## NAVIGATING THE SILENCE

# Tools for the Journey

I frequently use the phrase 'facing adversity' with the assumption that my readers are on the same page and have a shared understanding of what those words mean. We might share a mutual understanding of the phrase, but not necessarily.

Some people believe they are facing adversity when, in reality, they are trying to *escape* adversity in hopes of avoiding it altogether. In my experience, that usually isn't an option. When going around an obstacle isn't possible, sometimes I have to go through it, and depending on the adversity, that can be terrifying.

Whether a person's adversity is dealing with a painful hangnail or the unthinkable experience of the death of a child, turning away from the pain isn't an option. I might try to turn away and escape the pain by self-medicating, working 90 hours a week at work, or attempting to fill my thoughts with other things, but it never works, at least not for long. While an untreated hangnail might lead to an infection, the unprocessed loss of a child can eventually turn into an emotional implosion.

Implosions from a change in brain chemistry are similar to implosions from unaddressed trauma. Attempting to compartmentalize and shove our past traumas and painful experiences into a part of myself that I won't look at can eventually be even more explosive. The coping mechanism of compartmentalization is considered a form of dissociation[22], or what was previously referred to as multiple personalities. Regardless of how it is framed, it's not a healthy response.

### Letting go of the anger

Although I didn't let on to those around me since losing my ability to speak, I was angry about all that I had lost and endured. I was angry that the cancer had returned, angry that my dentist and new ENT didn't catch it, but mostly, I was angry that my life would never be the same.

When I feel anger, it is easy to focus that anger on something or someone. Who, or what, was I angry at? Where did I focus my vitriol? The doctors? God? My DNA? Or the COVID-19 vaccine? Microplastics in my water and food? Stress? Or myself for the choices I've made? Doctors are human, not all-seeing gods.

Letting go of anger will look different for everyone, and what worked for me may not work as well for others. What worked for me:

---

[22] Brown, R. J. (2006). Different Types of Dissociation Have Different Psychological Mechanisms. Trauma Dissociation, 7, 7-28.

**Talking about it**. I found that 'talking' (I wrote out my words) to a friend or one of my sisters helped me vent and allowed me a safe place to show my emotions. My talking also included talking to God. For extended conversations, I would go on solo walks, hikes, or bike rides. Venting my hurts, sadness, crushed dreams—all of it—was cathartic.

**Journaling**[23]. Writing down my thoughts daily or even a couple of times a week was healing as well. I know that the process of writing this book has been a part of my healing. Writing helps me process, especially loss or confusion. I've had to stop repeatedly to wipe away my tears so I could see what I'm writing. For me, putting my thoughts on the written page has been integral to purging my pain and sadness.

**Artistic outlets**. Painting or creating art has been a powerful way to relax my brain, giving me a break from overthinking, 'stewing,' and ruminating on those things I cannot change. Creating art helps keep my brain happy.

**Music**. Creating a playlist of songs that helped describe what I was going through was helpful. I recommend searching online for lyrics with keywords related to the experience or emotion. For the loss of a child, for example, I might include Eric Clapton's song, *Tears in Heaven*.

---

[23] Pennebaker, J. W. (2018). Expressive Writing in Psychological Science. Perspectives on Psychological Science, 13(2), 226-229. https://doi.org/10.1177/1745691617707315

**Physical activity**. I committed to some form of exercise every 3-5 days each week, which was a healthy approach to healing and letting go. Even as a young boy, when I was angry or overwhelmed, I would go outside and run until the tears stopped and I was too exhausted to run any further. By the time I got home, I was calm enough to process.

**Healthy distractions**. All of the above were healthy distractions for me. For others, I recommend taking up old or new hobbies, which can be a great way to distract and provide space for healing. I started making sourdough bread to distract myself from the disappointment I felt from rejection. I had a lot to 'unpack' and consider, so my bread-baking skills had many opportunities to improve. Volunteering can not only serve to distract but also help build relationships with others.

**Build a support system/network**. Although I've had a great 'tribe' of supporters to talk with, those without that kind of support can usually find it in support groups. These types of groups are available in most areas that focus on specific purposes, such as anger management, loss of a child, divorce, and others. I recommend searching online to find options in specific cities or counties. A list of suggestions is in the back of this book.

**Seek professional counseling**. Although talking about hurts with family and friends can be helpful for some, talking to a professional can be more productive for most people.

**Forgiveness.** Holding on to past hurts and pain can not only negatively affect the body but can also rob a person from finding peace in the present. Forgiving others, even if they didn't ask for it or I feel they don't deserve it, can help purge toxic emotions. This wasn't a one-time technique for me. I have to forgive constantly. That doesn't mean I need to go to someone's house and say, "I know what you did, and I forgive you," but making that decision in the quiet of my own thoughts has been powerful.

**Letting go.** Forgiveness is vital to the process of letting go, but the two aren't synonymous. Just because I forgive doesn't mean I automatically let loose the shackles of anger. For me, I chose to let go of my anger because it's toxic and seems to feed on itself. Unchecked, anger can take me down emotionally and physically, lead to increasingly dark thoughts, rob me of my joy, and drain me of my mental and emotional energy. However, letting go can help heal emotional wounds and open the door to experiencing joy again.

While the tools I relied on were crucial, the care and compassion of those around me played an equally important role. Reflecting on the kindness I experienced revealed just how much bedside manners can impact the healing process.

# Bedside Manners

When I was a boy, I remember hearing my mother talking with a friend about a doctor, I wasn't hanging on every word because I was doing 'kid stuff,' but my ears perked when Mom used the phrase "bedside manner." I continued to hear the phrase growing up, and it wasn't until I tore my meniscus playing racquetball in college that I truly learned the importance of physicians having excellent bedside manner skills.

I had purchased a new pair of racquetball shoes known for their incredible grip. The hype was true. While playing a game with a friend, I turned to face the front of the court, but my foot didn't. It stayed firmly planted, so when I twisted, it caused the cartilage in my knee to tear.

A buddy of mine helped me get in to see a sports doctor the next day, and from the moment he entered the examination room, my stress seemed to fade. The doctor shook my hand with a warm smile and sat on an exam stool so he could talk with me eye-to-eye. He told me that he was one of the first surgeons in the world to perform arthroscopic surgery when he repaired the injuries of soldiers in Vietnam. He explained how he would make three small incisions around my kneecap and insert a small camera to help him see as he worked. Rather than be in the hospital for days like I was in junior high school, I could walk as soon as the procedure was finished. He reminded me of how Joan Benoit qualified for the 1984 Summer Olympics in Los Angeles by winning the U.S. Olympic Women's Marathon Trials in my hometown of Olympia just a year earlier. Joan achieved that feat just 17 days after having an arthroscopic on her knee and went on to win her race at the Olympics.

The surgeon took all the time I needed to understand what had happened in my knee, what needed to be done, why he was the best surgeon for my case, and how he was going to make my knee "as good as new." His confidence, backed by a calming voice, was my first experience with seeing a good 'bedside manner' in action.

Years later, when I was a medical myotherapist, I occasionally referred patients to a surgeon in Olympia who was exceptionally skilled but had the personality of a grumpy old man. I had to warn those I referred by saying, "His demeanor might be a bit off-putting, but he is the best at what he does."

I shouldn't have had to preface my referrals with excuses for the surgeon's behavior, but there were many more like him. Maybe if medical schools and residency programs taught a course of study on calming patients, we would have less road rage.

After all of the many surgeries I've had and all of the physicians I've had caring for me, those with empathy have made the road to healing easier to process. I remember first meeting Dr. Xingwei Sui of Group Health's oncology department. Dr. Sui was an exceptional doctor who was quick to offer a big smile and a two-handed handshake. When he entered my exam room on my first visit, he greeted me and put his hand on my shoulder. With a warm, assuring smile and a thick Chinese accent, he said, "Robert, I am going to take care of you. It will not be easy, but I will help you through this." There was something about his gentle spirit that both comforted me and gave me hope.

If a patient is an emotional wreck when they are given a lung cancer diagnosis, a doctor could say, "I'm so sorry. I know this must be really difficult to process." OR they could say, "You've been smoking for 30 years! What did you expect was going to happen?!"

I had friends say they wished my boss would get cancer so they could have empathy for what I had endured. I may have been 'done wrong' or treated harshly, as some saw it, but I wouldn't wish what I've experienced on my worst enemy. My radiologist said something similar back in 2013, before I was to begin my 30 high-dose radiation treatments. She said, "Bob, your cancer is aggressive, and I need to give you the most amount of radiation I can prescribe without killing you. I'm not going to soft-sell this, but it will be difficult, and you'll feel like the insides of your mouth have been cut by razor blades. It's going to be horrible. I wouldn't even do this to my worst enemy." That brutal honesty came from a place of empathetic caring.

Our friends and family might be able to show sympathy, but the doctor has the opportunity to show empathy. Note: If a friend is going through something similar to what I've gone through, I need to do my best not to one-up them with a "mine was worse" story.

In his book Blink, *The Power of Thinking Without Thinking*, Malcolm Gladwell discusses the frequency of doctors who were sued for surgical errors compared to how much empathy they showed their patients.

Gladwell says the chance of a doctor being sued doesn't depend on how many mistakes they make. While some skilled doctors get sued often, others who make mistakes never do, and most patients harmed by negligence don't sue at all. It turns out that lawsuits aren't just about poor medical care but also about how patients are treated.

Ultimately, Gladwell found that patients are more likely to sue if they feel ignored, rushed, or poorly treated by their doctor. People rarely sue doctors they like, even if mistakes happen. Kindness and respect go a long way in avoiding lawsuits.

Experience can bring wisdom if we let it—at least, I would like to think so. However, wisdom does not always go hand in hand with intelligence, especially *emotional intelligence.*

Doctors, especially doctors who work with cancer patients, have the difficult job of 'being bearers of bad news.

I was fortunate to have had emotionally intelligent physicians who showed caring and empathy when telling me I had cancer, the cancer had returned, or that my entire tongue would have to be removed to save my life. Having to deliver challenging, life-shattering news on a regular basis could easily lead to being calloused and unfeeling. If doctors are disconnected and try to fake empathy, their patients will know better. For me, I needed to hear the whole truth.

No doctor has made me any promises that weren't true. No assurances I won't die from this cancer I've been challenged with since 2008—16 years at the time of this writing. I've only been given the truth about what I could expect. In 2013, my radiologist told me that the radiation and chemotherapy would extend my life by another 10 years, and she was right. The wisdom she had learned from experience would give me another decade—a ten-year life extension. When the cancer returned in 2023, I wasn't given any words of hope.

Receiving an additional 50 radiation treatments on top of the 'lifetime maximum' I received in 2013 was aggressive. There is scientific certainty that the significant doses I received will bring side effects in the coming months and years. I see the physiological changes in my body. Beyond worrying about the surety of death is the fact that the radiation has also allowed me to continue living for now. None of us are guaranteed a long life. I feel uniquely blessed that I've experienced things and had opportunities few others have had. I've lived a full life, and that's all I need. There is a verse in the Bible that says, "Anyone who loves their life will lose it, while anyone who hates their life in this world will keep it for eternal life." - John 12:25[24]. That doesn't mean that if I love my life that God is going to take it away. Everyone loses their life. It is a reminder that our time here on earth has an expiration date.

Although I have had some exceptional doctors and nurses over the years, I have to clarify that I have been an anatomy, physiology, and pathology educator. In other words, I know a great deal about how the body is constructed and what can go wrong with it. I also understand medical terminology, allowing me to converse with medical professionals as colleagues of sorts. This knowledge has given me an advantage that most pa-

---

[24] John 12:25, New International Version Bible

tients don't have, and I have received better-than-aver-
age care as a result.

Patients who don't always feel heard when navigating
medical care should know that self-advocacy is key. If a
doctor isn't listening or dismisses concerns, seeking a
second opinion or another physician is essential. Rude
or unhelpful staff, such as nurses or aids, can be re-
placed upon request, and hospital social workers can
provide support when advocacy feels overwhelming.
Patients should also thoroughly research treatments
and medications and refuse anything they feel is not
right. If their requests for alternative therapies are met
with skepticism, they should respectfully present evi-
dence-based studies to make their case. Patients who
empower themselves with knowledge and persistence
can significantly improve their quality of care.

While doctors get the kudos for saving lives, I've
learned that nurses are the 'secret sauce' to post-surgery
recovery. Whether it was talking me down from an
emotional cliff in the ICU, holding my hand while I
sobbed from overwhelming pain, or offering a radiant
smile in the morning, nurses have blessed me the most.

In a normal doctor-patient relationship, there is a
professional boundary where the patient shares personal issues, but the doctor keeps up a professional fence,
leaving their home life at the door. I've found that when
interacting with nurses, especially when I get to com-

municate with them 24 hours a day, seven days a week for two weeks, we get to know each other. I tend to ask a lot of questions when I meet people, and that has been true with the hospital nurses and therapists. Before long, I knew about their training, their families, what sports their kids were involved in, and eventually, about their relationships, broken dreams, and struggles they had faced in life. It probably would be frowned upon by their bosses, but that connection reduced my stress, gave me a trustworthy sounding board when I was concerned about something, or feel heard when I needed to vent.

Ultimately, the best nurses—bar none—have been the ones who hummed and sang as they entered my room. Their joy in their work was always contagious and healing.

Experiencing compassion from caregivers reminded me of the value of straightforward advice. My father's no-nonsense perspective became something I leaned on, offering clarity and strength during difficult times.

## How My Father Sees It

*Bob, when you told me you had cancer back in 2008, I was concerned, of course. But I didn't let fear take over. Instead, I did what I've always done when life throws something heavy at us—I trusted God to take care of things. Worrying never fixes anything, so I just prayed and believed we'd get through it together as a family. It wasn't easy to hear, but I knew you were strong, and I figured that with faith, you'd find your way through.*

*If I've learned anything from watching you on this journey, it's this: don't give up. Even when things feel impossible, you keep going. And that's my advice for the people around someone facing something like this: show up and be there for them. You don't have to fix it; you have to care. Family means everything in times like these.*

*Looking back, I have so many fond memories of you as a child, but a couple always come to mind. Like the time you decided to race your skateboard down the sidewalk and accidentally sent it crashing through the basement window. You said, "Well, that didn't go as planned." So, I taught you how to replace the pane with glazing putty. I figured you might as well learn something from it—and you did. Then there's the spading fork incident—you know, the one that went straight through your foot. Not exactly your*

*best moment, but you stayed calm, and I was proud of you for that. You didn't let panic take over, and that's always been something I admire about you—your ability to face tough moments head-on.*

*If I get to Heaven before you, here's what I want you to know: keep the faith. Life's not always fair, but don't stop trusting God or believing in what's good. Keep going to church, and don't give up, even when life makes it tempting.*

*Bob, I don't always say it, but I'm proud of you —more than you'll ever know. You've shown so much strength through this, and it's been something to witness. I may not have all the words, but I hope you know how much I love you.*

*With all my love,*
*Dad*

My father's direct approach helped me face the realities of my situation head-on, but nothing could fully prepare me for the challenge of navigating a world where I could no longer use my voice.

# Being Mute in a Speaking World

Those who know me know I love technology—a lot. As a kid, I saved my paper route money to buy all kinds of gadgets. As an adult, I've been a frequent attendee at the Consumer Electronics Show (CES) in Las Vegas, a virtual toyland for guys like me. In tech terms, I'm known as an 'early adopter' in that I have my home wired up with two Amazon Alexa Echos, a Google Nest Video screen, and smart switches and bulbs on nearly every outlet in my house. I have an Amazon Fire TV, Apple TV, and Comcast's xFinity X1 recording box. I'm also in the 'Apple universe' in that I have an Apple iWatch and the newest iPhone, which allows me to access the new Apple Intelligence platform. The problem for me is that all of the devices above are best used by speaking to them.

Each morning, before losing my speech, I'd walk into the kitchen and say, "Alexa, good morning," and the Echo on the counter would say good morning, turn on pre-selected lights, tell me the weather, and then start playing a string of news reports. I can't do that anymore.

I realize that not having lights that turn on and off as my voice commands is a 'first world problem' and silly when compared to more critical issues facing humanity. One of the things that is most scary for me is not being able to speak if I have to push the S.O.S. Button in my car. If I need help, I can't speak to the operator at OnStar.

I hadn't thought about it at first, but our world is becoming a hands-free society with all types of technology based on voice interactions. If you've ever called a company's customer service number for support and encountered their automated 'phone tree,' you know what I mean. When the voice prompts me to say what I'm calling about, I feel like I'm playing a virtual game of charades, but the automated system can't see me or understand me.

One of the most challenging changes for me—as someone who previously talked for a living—is the silence when with other people. I can't fill uncomfortable quiet with idle chatter, and people must patiently wait for me to write down my thoughts and responses, making conversations less fluid and natural.

Years ago, a friend accused me of having my eyes glaze over when we were talking because I was thinking of what I was going to say next rather than listening and taking the time to hear them. I learned about 'active listening' in my college communications courses but didn't practice it. There is nothing like losing my ability to speak to help me keep my ears open during conversations. Now, when someone is talking, I can't write down what I want to say without revealing that I'm no longer listening. Not an option. I have to listen, think about my response, and then write my response down.

Due to the time it takes to handwrite my message, I have to keep each response brief and short enough to fit on the board—legibly. Being forced to improve my handwriting has proven to be a challenge all on its own.

I can no longer communicate with my parents as I drive them to their appointments unless I pull the car over and write down my words.

I think what scares me most is losing my ability to communicate with my mother. She can't decipher my verbal attempts at talking. Few can. The problem is that Mom is losing her vision. She's been blind in her left eye since childhood, but her right eye is on a steady path of eventual blindness. When that day comes, I will need an interpreter or an emissary to decipher my handwriting and relay the message to her. Hopefully, technology can keep up with our need to communicate, but for now, my communication is limited to writing on a small dry-erase board, a "Boogie Board," or with paper and pen.

Left: The sticker on the back of my writing boards.
Right: My portable Boogie Board.

I wasn't sure what to expect out in public after recovering from surgery or how to navigate everyday encounters with strangers. When I am with others, it's not a problem, as they can speak for me. For example, when I take my parents through the Arby's drive-through, I have to open my window and have my Mom or Dad yell out their order from inside the car. It's a little comical to watch.

In public, I can get away with smiles and thumbs-up responses in most situations, but when someone asks me a straight-up question, things can get a little dicey unless I have a writing board handy. When I was going to my daily treatments at the Virginia Mason Hospital in downtown Seattle, a woman who was disheveled and appeared to be hopped up on some drug approached me. Her face and body twitched as she asked, "Do you know where the methadone clinic is? I need some. Do you know?" I paused because I didn't have my writing board.

For the record, my voice is perfect in my head. My tongue can move around my mouth and form words... the same way a double-leg amputee can feel their feet. When I spoke to her, though, all she heard was a mumbling man whose words didn't make any sense. I fumbled with my iPhone to search for the clinic, but she got frustrated and yelled, "Never mind," over her shoulder as she walked away.

Approaching people, whether I'm asking for directions from a stranger who's walking down the sidewalk or asking a fellow shopper if they know where the shoe department is, always draws an initial reaction. It's different for everyone. Some people's eyes widen in surprise, while others take a step back. Holding up that board makes me feel like a limo driver at the airport holding a sign with their passenger's last name. Speaking of which, on my last trip to Phoenix, a driver held up a sign with two last names reading, "Bacon/Slapper." I couldn't help but laugh out loud as I walked past him. The idea of someone slapping bacon still makes me chuckle. But I digress...

Image depicting an actual event recreated with
DALL·E, OpenAI's image generation tool.

While writing this book, I have also been searching for my next job in a communications-related position. Although I personalized every cover letter, I included a common paragraph that revealed I could no longer speak. I spun it as a positive, of course. In the cover letters, I wrote:

*"One of the personal experiences that profoundly shaped my perspective and approach to communication was losing my ability to speak due to cancer in 2023. While this experience presented many challenges, it has only strengthened my commitment to clear and effective communication. It has given me an even deeper under-*

*standing of the importance of inclusion, accessibility, and adaptability in delivering messages that resonate with diverse audiences. I continue to thrive in my professional roles by leveraging technology, written communication, and collaboration to ensure my voice is heard, even if not in the traditional sense."*

Among the many jobs I applied for was a position in a Washington State agency. The duties listed in the job posting orbited around a wide range of communications, including speaking to the press. The good news is that I received an email reply from the agency's human resources coordinator, who asked me how I thought I could do my job without speaking. The woman's email started a back-and-forth conversation, and I was eventually scheduled for an interview. Ultimately, I was thanked for applying, but they had hired someone else. No matter how I crafted my cover letter statements or how I answered interviewers' questions in Zoom interview chat windows, I had heard that same response from 47 companies and agencies: "Thanks for applying, but we've hired someone else."

Navigating my new reality of speech loss has been tricky. Still, it has forced me into new and uncomfortable situations, which can only serve to grow my 'emotional intelligence' and empathy for those with physical differences from what society calls normal. The minority will always be considered as different.

There is a series on Apple+ called See. The show is set in the far future when humankind has lost its sense of sight. "Jason Momoa stars as the father of twins with the 'mythic' ability to see[25]..." Imagine being one of only two people with vision when everyone else is blind. To be different or held in contempt by society for what makes me different.

The thought of being different and how that could affect a person came to me in childhood from a special animated show[26] called The Point[27] about a 'pointless' boy, Oblio, and his dog, Arrow. Everyone in the village has a pointed head except the round-headed Oblio. To hide his difference, he had to wear a pointed cap since birth to fit in. It's a cute story, but it got me thinking early on about being different and likely helped prepare me for today, where I am among a tiny group of people who've lost the ability to speak after taking a lifetime of their speaking ability for granted. I am still in the process of coming to terms with being different. Perhaps that's why Me and My Arrow[28], the theme song to The Point still rings in my head all of these many years later.

The good news is that most people are incredibly helpful and willing to take a moment to communicate

---

[25] https://tinyurl.com/yuv7nzc3

[26] https://www.youtube.com/watch?v=V6Qnd5vnpN0

[27] https://en.wikipedia.org/wiki/The_Point!

[28] "Me and My Arrow" by Harry Nilsson, from the album "The Point!," RCA Victor, 1971

with me. Once they read the *"I can hear you, but I am unable to speak"* sticker on the back of my writing board, their tone of voice and body language manifest a sweet attitude of generosity. That alone gives me hope in humanity amidst all of the impatience and annoyance in the world today.

Deafness is the number one birth defect in the U.S., which gives families the opportunity and time to learn American Sign Language, or ASL. However, families of adults who lose their ability to speak don't typically know how to use sign language, nor does the person who lost their ability to speak, making communication with their families and those in their communities a significant challenge. I know that has been true for me.

Society as a whole isn't designed for the non-verbal, and while I've heard endless references over the past few years about 'Diversity, Equity, and Inclusion,' the reality is that philosophy doesn't apply to everyone. My hope is that my loss of speech has begun to impact society in general and shine a light on the struggles of mute individuals. The mute are not helpless but forced to be adaptable and resilient. I hope that I can work as an advocate for the mute and increase accessibility options for personal and on-the-job use.

This statement will sound a bit dated at some point in the future, but I have faith that artificial intelligence (AI) and other technologies can be used in tandem to give the mute their voices back. Changes are coming, and AI is already able to take samples of my voice and realistically synthesize it for presentation use. If all goes the way I envision, we will be able to translate brainwaves into an AI text-to-speech module on a wearable speaker for real-time, in-person conversations.

Navigating life without the ability to speak forced me to reevaluate how I communicate and connect with others. Amidst the silence, I began to search for a deeper meaning of my profound loss.

# In Search of Meaning

Adversity doesn't necessarily have a meaning, and thinking there is some underlying meaning can often lead people to conjure up something based on their desire to find meaning.

When a group of friends are involved in an accident where their SUV veered off the road and crashed into a tree, each might interpret the event differently based on their belief system and how it lines up compared to their previous experiences. The driver believes it was a sign he should go to rehab to stop drinking, another friend thinks it was a sign he should run for mayor to improve the street lighting, and another believes it happened because they weren't supposed to attend the concert they were driving to. While each reason could be valid, it is more likely because they traveled too fast for the conditions, and the tree was simply there.

I've been asked several times about my attitude and why I'm not mad about my string of adversities. Of course, I felt anger, but rather than linger on that emotion, I needed to break adversity down into parts and give the parts some contemplative thought. For me, using logic has been a powerful tool.

When horrible things happen, some will angrily ask, "Why would a 'loving God' allow this to happen to me?" They get furious at God because He didn't keep "bad" from happening in this world. Logic has kept me from letting my initial anger transition into the furious stage. The truth is that humans have free will—the ability to make choices that affect their future. People have choices that, in turn, have consequences—with each choice setting into motion chains of events with far-reaching ripple effects culminating in both positive and negative outcomes. Yet many blame God even though a negative outcome ultimately resulted from decisions made by other humans. Accidents happen, and chains of events lead to peril.

Remember that Carrie Underwood song, *Jesus Take the Wheel*? If humans genuinely wanted to keep bad things from happening on this earth, they would have to relinquish their freedom of choice—their free will. Short of doing that, God shouldn't be blamed for many of the bad things that happen. For example, let's say a man is craving a big, greasy burger, so he gets into his car and heads out to the nearest burger joint. Meanwhile, God knows his greasy burger habit will lead to cardiovascular disease. Suddenly, the steering wheel overrides his input, and the car drives itself to a nearby vegan restaurant. Should he be angry? Given a choice, would he be willing to give up the freedom of free will? Does he *really* want God to take the wheel or answer his prayers to stay healthy? People want free will yet will still blame the negative consequences of their choices on God.

True, some blame can rest on our shoulders, like a parent wanting to blame God because their daughter is dead. Still, they won't be accountable and accept responsibility for demonstrating a life of alcohol-related mishaps in front of their daughter, who eventually thought it would be okay to drive under the influence.

### Looking for Meaning

Ultimately, an event's meaning is what a person decides it is. Perhaps I shouldn't spend time searching for an event's underlying meaning; instead, I should come to terms with the fact that it happened and then redirect my focus to the blessings and gifts the experience has allowed into my life.

Did I do something to deserve cancer? After receiving my cancer diagnosis, several people said things to me that were both hurtful and untrue. One well-meaning friend said, "It must be because there is sin in your life." Another told me, "There is cancer in your tongue because there is something that you aren't confessing—a truth you haven't spoken." Another said, "There is someone you haven't forgiven—you must forgive. You have cancer because of your unforgiving heart!" The fact is, none of those things were true. Sometimes, bad things happen to good people, just as *the rain falls on the just and the unjust*[29].

Looking for meaning can get out of control and sometimes be an unhealthy exercise. I know people who always look for the negative and worst-case scenarios and others who have a positive outlook and assume the best until proven otherwise. For example, let's say someone's spouse has been working late the past few nights and explains they are doing so because they have a proposal deadline, and missing it will impact a potential promotion. Their spouse can either assume they are telling the truth or worry that they are having an illicit affair with someone at work. One is a healthy thought, and the other is disturbing, with the latter possibly spilling over into a negative and disturbing place, ultimately affecting the relationship.

Cognitive Reframing, a tool used in Cognitive Behavioral Therapy[30] (CBT), is generally invoked around issues requiring changing negative thought patterns. In CBT, the therapist helps the patient learn to identify negative thought patterns so they can work to change them. However, I also used this purposeful process to change how I viewed events in my life. Taking out a pad of paper and a pen and finding a quiet place to think

---

[29] Matthew 5:45, Holy Bible
[30] https://www.amazon.com/Cognitive-Behavioural-Therapy-Dummies-Willson/dp/1119601126

can work wonders in looking for the upsides of our adversity.

CBT focuses on the relationship between thoughts, emotions, and behaviors rather than a specific situation or incident. By recognizing and changing unhelpful or distorted thought processes, people can improve and regulate how they respond. In short, it is about how feelings affect behaviors and how behaviors affect feelings.

I interviewed Casey Ward, PsyD, a cognitive behavioral therapist in Washington State, who said that we can refocus on what is essential by compartmentalizing. Casey explained,

*"Being able to focus is a natural gift we all have, but how many of us have the ability to refocus? That is a skill you have to develop and takes practice. It's what I work with many athletes on, and it's what you have to work on if you're dealing with adversity. For example, if I am distracted by what's currently going on in my life, if I'm thinking I don't have any money, or I don't have anything to eat, I'm failing at work, or my parents are getting a divorce, those sources of anxiety can put me in a tailspin where none of my challenges get resolved, and I just want to forget about them all. How do I refocus? Notice the whole picture, including the accompanying emotion, and let it reside in the background of*

*your mind, but pick the most important issue(s) to start with and bring it to the foreground by addressing it systematically from a place of alert attention--mindfulness if you will. It takes practice."*

How does someone survive when they've lost something or someone important to them? How do they endure unthinkable adversity?

I mentioned previously about processing thoughts of suicide and the fact that I am a logical thinker. This has been true when it has involved my business issues, life, relationships, and when dealing with adversity. When I used Cognitive Reframing, I thought about a problem and purposely found a new way to interpret it. For me, this tool has been a lifesaver.

As I explored my life's purpose, it was clear that meaning often comes down to a choice: whether to let adversity define us or to use it as an opportunity for growth. This decision was key to my journey forward.

## Bitter or Better?

Choosing to be grateful when in the throws of hardship might sound counter-intuitive. In my case, loss has forced me to take inventory of the blessings I still have. Loss also clears away the things that obscure my view of the many blessings I have.

If you can, stop reading for a moment and list ten blessings you have right now.   If that seems difficult, start with five. These don't even have to be obvious blessings. For some, it might start with our basic needs, like having a roof over our heads, a mattress, clean water, or a warm meal at the Salvation Army.

As Viktor Frankl said, our ability to choose how we react can never be taken from us. I can respond angrily that I have lost my tongue, or I can be thankful that I am alive and am loved.

Although I have lost my sense of taste, let alone my ability to eat anything by mouth, I have gained time by no longer having to shop for food, cook or prepare complicated meals, clean up afterward, or worry about gaining weight. Don't get me wrong. I MISS FOOD, but I haven't lost the memories of taste. I can still close my eyes and enjoy whatever I choose. I can recall my favorite foods' taste, texture, and lingering flavors, such as deep dish BBQ chicken and bacon pizza from Papa Murphy's, pralines and cream ice cream with thick caramel sauce poured on top—a blue-rare filet mignon, tender Teriyaki chicken or buttered and salted corn on the cob. I will never be able to experience food again, but that's okay. There are a lot more things worth worrying about than the taste of food.

Several years before my cancer diagnosis, I was in New York City for a training course on providing medical massage treatments for cancer patients. Located on Manhatten's upper eastside is a cluster of buildings that make up Memorial Sloan Kettering Hospital, arguably the foremost medical center for cancer treatments. As I walked from my lodging at the Helmsley Medical Tower, my ears rang from the non-stop chorus of ambulance sirens wailing, taking patients to one of the many nearby hospitals, including the Cornell Graduate School of Medical Sciences, NY Presbyterian, and others.

On the last training day, we accompanied the lead oncology massage therapist on her rounds, meeting her cancer patients. Toward the end of her shift, we approached the room of an elderly gentleman. His nurse shared in a low voice that the man was recovering from a recent surgery that had removed part of his throat, and he was in a great deal of pain. She then signaled us to join her and her patient.

Sitting up in bed was an elderly black man who had flown in from out of state for treatment. As we entered the room, he fumbled with his shirt as he slowly buttoned it up. The nurse asked, "How are we doing today, Mr. Washington?" He took some time to clear his throat and position himself to answer her question. It only took a minute before he could eventually speak, but watching him struggle felt like an eternity. Finally, with a gentle smile across his face and with a strained and raspy voice, Mr. Washington said just three words: *"I am blessed."*

I got choked up hearing his words and couldn't stop the tears running down my face. He had suffered so much but was still thankful. How was that possible? His smile continued to glow even though he was in obvious pain.

At the time, I had no idea that Mr. Washington's words would exemplify an attitude of gratitude and blessing and serve as an example for me to follow someday. I then made a conscious decision that, should I ever find myself in a similar situation, I would emulate Mr. Washington's attitude and look for the blessings in my life.

Occasionally, when I look at myself in the mirror these days, I see a man with a permanently disfigured body living in the aftermath of cancer. The words Mr. Washington spoke those decades ago still ring fresh in my ears—words that now hold a great deal of meaning for me. Thanks to his example, I smile, knowing that regardless of my circumstances and despite my scars, *I am blessed.*

Choosing to be better rather than bitter helped me extract important lessons from my experiences. These insights—both hard-earned and deeply personal—would become the foundation for a lifetime of wisdom.

# PART FIVE

## LESSONS LEARNED

## Lessons for a Lifetime

Life is one long empirical experience. Experience I've learned from, and that has helped me grow in wisdom when I've been open to it. I haven't always learned my lesson the first time around. For me, the lessons I've learned from my experiences have consistently helped others, and I've been honored to share my insights with them. My life's twists, turns, and obstacles have helped me gain insights and wisdom to navigate each new challenge as it comes, even if those challenges come in rapid succession, knocking me down before I can get my footing. The following are the lessons I've learned during my journies with adversities and truths I have often shared with others.

### Adversity Shapes Us

Adversity can be painful and be a transformative shock to everything we know to be true, testing our beliefs, friendships, and perspectives. It can strip away our sense of security and help us understand what is truly important to us. Adversity has taken my voice, but it has given me resilience and clarified my purpose.

### Forgiveness Frees Us

Holding onto anger or bitterness is like drinking poison and expecting the other person to suffer. Forgiveness doesn't excuse another's hurtful actions or words, but it frees us from their power over us. As we forgive others and ourselves, we can find the freedom to heal and grow.

### Perspective is a Choice

Although life brings adversities beyond our control, how we view and interpret them is up to us. We get to choose how we see our losses and obstacles. We can either wallow in our loss or view it as an opportunity to grow. My shift from "Why me?" to "Why not me?" has transformed my relationship with adversity and allowed me to hold on to what remains rather than perpetually grieve what is gone.

### Adversity Builds Gratitude

The people and things I've lost have made me more grateful for those people and things I still have. Losing my ability to eat has helped me see the social blessings of sharing a meal. Losing my voice helped me discover the power of writing. Thankfulness and gratitude, even for the smallest of things, can transform despair into hope.

### Preparation Eases Transition
Coming to terms with what lies ahead can make it easier to endure. I've recorded messages for my daughters, recorded my lectures for continuity, and contemplated my own mortality. While we can't control everything, preparation gives us a sense of control, peace, and clarity of purpose.

### Empathy is Crucial
Genuine empathy requires presence and understanding rather than just words. Through my experiences, I've learned the power of simply being there for others—to listen without judgment and show compassion without platitudes.

### Adaptation is Strength
When life takes something from us, we can either resist or adapt. I've learned to use writing tablets, embraced numerous types of digital communication, and found new ways to connect with others. Adaptation isn't about giving up but finding another way forward.

### Resilience is a Muscle
We aren't born with resilience. Resilience is built over time through repeated challenges and adversities and by observing others who've gone before us. Each set-

back has been an opportunity to strengthen my determination, grow my patience, and remind myself that I can endure far more than I could have imagined.

## Time is Precious

Facing a shortened life expectancy has made it clear that I must treasure every moment. I need to invest my time with family, look for opportunities to connect, and look at each encounter with others as an opportunity to change a life. Life isn't about how much time we have left but how we use it.

## Vulnerability is Courageous

Sharing my struggles, fears, and darkest moments has been terrifying and liberating. Allowing myself to be vulnerable opens the door for connection and allows others to see not only my fortitude but also how my experiences helped to grow and shape my resilience and humanity.

## Support Systems Matter

'It takes a village.' Nobody can—or should—face adversity alone. Family, friends, coworkers, and even strangers have played crucial roles in my survival and healing. If you are struggling, don't hesitate to reach out. Beyond friends or family, there are volunteers, professionals, and support groups who also want to support you.

## Grief and Change are Inevitable

Experiencing grief isn't limited to just the death of someone we care about. I've grieved my speaking and singing voice, my former appearance, and my ease of living. Just as the Greek philosopher Heraclitus said, "The only constant in life is change, and learning to navigate it with grace is one of the greatest skills we can cultivate."

## Faith Provides Comfort

My faith has been an anchor, reminding me that I am never truly alone and my life is part of a larger plan. It doesn't erase the pain or promise me physical healing, but it gives me a steady presence through the storms and gives me reassurance and strength.

## Advocacy is Powerful

Sharing my story has allowed me to raise awareness for others facing similar challenges. I've found purpose in being a voice for the voiceless, including advocating for cancer patients, the mute community, or those with disabilities.

## Purpose Transcends Adversity

Losing my speaking ability didn't take away my ability to communicate, teach, or encourage. Our life's purpose isn't tied to a single ability, role, or vocation. It evolves with us. Alexander Graham Bell said, "When one door closes, another door opens, but we often look so long and so regretfully upon the closed door that we do not see the ones which open for us." And I say, if you don't see another door, buy a chainsaw. Sometimes, our only advocate is ourselves.

### Self-Care is Essential

Healing isn't just physical—it's mental, emotional, and spiritual. To regain strength, it is imperative to take adequate time to rest, reflect, and care for yourself. Self-care isn't selfish; it's survival. Be good to yourself.

### Life is Unpredictable

All plans are guidelines, not guarantees. Even in construction, there are blueprints and as-built plans which detail how it was actually built. Nearly every building's as-built plans are slightly different than what was intended at the outset of the construction project, and this is true in life as well. If it weren't, I would be an astronaut right now. Life will throw countless twists and turns in business, health, and personal lives, and expecting the unexpected will help you take the opportunity to pivot.

### Creative Solutions Can Work

The Greek philosopher Plato said, "Necessity is the mother of invention." Thinking outside the box, from recording my lectures to creating video resumes, has allowed me to adapt and thrive despite limitations.

### Advancing Despite Loss

The loss of my voice could have silenced me, but I found new ways to communicate and be heard. Loss doesn't define us, but how we respond to it does. The path forward is there, but you may not recognize it initially, and it will likely look different than you imagined.

### Acceptance of Mortality

Coming to terms with the fact that life is finite has given me a greater appreciation for the here and now. Rather than fearing death, we must celebrate the opportunities that life brings with it.

These lessons I've learned are not the product of an easy life. They are the rewards of struggles, reflections, and growth when adversity had stripped away the comforts I once took for granted. I offer them to you not as a prescription but as a perspective—one that has allowed me to find strength in silence, hope in hardship, and purpose in adversity. Your path and experiences will be different from mine. What has worked for me may not work for you, and that's normal. When you allow yourself to learn and grow from struggles, you unlock a strength that no challenge can take away.

I've written about these lessons to be a companion on your journey—not a map but a guide, not a cure but a comfort. They are my way of saying: You are not alone, and your story is far from over. There is strength in silence, hope in hardship, and purpose in every step forward. The journey is yours, but I am here to remind you—it's a journey worth taking.

The lessons I had gathered over the years weren't just for me—they were meant to be shared. Writing a letter to my grandson allowed me to pass on what I had learned and offer guidance for his own path through life.

# A Letter to My Grandson

My desire to encourage others isn't specific. Whether it is a homeless person, an elderly neighbor, or a high school football team, we all need encouragement and can be blessed by the shared wisdom of those who've gone before us. This is especially true when it comes to our children and grandchildren. With that in mind, this letter is to my grandson, Roman:

*Dear Roman,*

*As I write this, I can't help but think about all the things I hope for you in your life. You're only four years old right now and too young to fully understand the words I'm about to share, but someday, when you're ready, I hope you'll see them as a guide and a reminder of how deeply your grandpa loves you.*

*Roman, life will bring incredible joy. You'll find laughter with friends who stand by you, love in unexpected places, and triumphs that make you feel invincible. But life will also challenge you. It will test your strength and your determination, and there will be moments when you feel like giving up. Those are the moments I want to speak to.*

*When you face struggles—and you will—remember that the pain you feel is not the end of your story. It is part of your journey, just one chapter in a book that is still being written. Ad-*

*versity will teach you lessons that no amount of comfort ever could. It will show you your strength and the marvel of resilience.*

*As you will come to know, I've faced my share of challenges in my lifetime. Losing my voice to cancer was one of the hardest things I've ever endured. There were days when I felt the weight of it all pressing down on me, and I wasn't sure how I'd move forward or what my future would look like. But I learned something through that pain, and that is that life isn't about what we lose but what we choose to do with what remains.*

*Grandson, you have more strength within you than you realize. There will be times when life feels unfair or overwhelming, but I want you to know that you are never alone. You carry within you a legacy of resilience, of family, and of love. Lean on the people who love you, never be afraid to ask for help, and seek God's will through prayer.*

*Most importantly, never stop believing in yourself. You are capable of greatness—not because of what you achieve, but because of the person you are. Be kind, be courageous, and always strive to make the world a little brighter for those around you.*

*Remember, even in the silence, your voice matters. Your actions, your kindness, and your per-*

*sistence will leave an impact far greater than words ever could.*

*I love you with all my heart, Roman, and I am proud to call you my grandson. No matter where life takes you, know that I am with you, cheering you on and that my love for you is unshakable.*

*With all my love,*

*Grandpa (Papa Bob)*

In writing to my grandson, I realized how much thought goes into finding the right words. It made me reflect on the importance of what we say—and what we shouldn't say—when supporting others navigating struggles of their own.

## What to Say and Not to Say

While going through the worst of my challenges, I appreciated it when people would visit and talk about the good things happening in their lives and the stresses and challenges they were facing. It allowed me to take my mind off my problems and offer my thoughts (if they wanted my advice.) Hearing others tell me they had gone through something similar yet 'much worse' than mine wasn't helpful. 'One-upping' someone with an 'Oh yeah? I had it worse when...' type of story, while I was in the throws of adversity, wasn't beneficial, but a listening ear from a true friend was.

First and foremost, I was thankful for friends who could 'listen' when I was most overwhelmed by adversity, and when they spoke, they ensured they were helping rather than hindering my mental state. People can be ignorant about what to say to someone who is going through or has experienced adversity. There are things friends can say and things that should never be said, including:

**What should never be said to someone facing adversity:**

- **"You're going to be fine."** Why? Nobody truly knows that for sure; it sounds superficial and meaningless.

- **"Everything happens for a reason."** Why? Although good may ultimately come from the situation, thinking God gave you cancer isn't comforting and doesn't align with the sacred texts of most faiths.

- **"What do you need me to do for you?"** Why? For someone in the throes of adversity, even the energy expended while trying to think of what you can do can be exhausting. Likely, they don't even know what they need—so they shouldn't be made to think about it. Instead, having someone go ahead and straighten up my house, do some cleaning, or do my laundry without being asked was a relief. Unexpected books to read or a stack of magazines was nice, too.

- **"Tell me all of the details! How did it happen? Did it hurt? Can I see it?"** Why? They've likely been asked those painful questions before, and each time they are forced to retell it, they have to relive every detail of the dreadful moment. They will explain in their own time if they want others to know their personal details.

- **"It's not that bad. You've got insurance."**
  Why? Making this type of statement is dismissing the immeasurable impact of the event—the time, expense, and inconvenience of getting back to normal again and minimizing the losses incurred, disruption to their lives, and potential PTSD from the event itself.

**Things you should never say to someone fighting cancer:**

- **"That's why I never use antiperspirant. It gives you cancer, you know."** Why? We shouldn't dole out advice on how to avoid cancer or offer our insights on what must have caused it. Our bodies all respond differently to different things, and ultimately, getting cancer can be due to the luck of the draw. The onus shouldn't be placed on the victim/patient.

- **"You have to stop eating sugar!"** Why? Non-professionals shouldn't give nutritional advice. Many of the theories online are often baseless and unproven. Plus, certain foods or supplements can adversely affect any ongoing treatments. Different bodies respond to things differently. Finally, avoid making someone feel they are to blame for their misfortune.

- **"Any of us could get hit by a car in the crosswalk tomorrow."** Why? It's true; anyone could. But don't diminish what they are experiencing now by discussing what could happen to someone else later.

- **"Miracles happen!"** Why? This colloquialism can result in a range of responses. The patient most often hears the unspoken subtext: "You're going to need a miracle."

- **"It happened to my uncle, but he was way worse."** Why? Making comparisons to other people's experiences is meaningless and dismissive.

- **"I'm just too busy to visit. Sorry."** Why? Don't avoid a friend or loved one because you won't know what to say or because you're uncomfortable being around someone who's been through a catastrophe. They need their friends. Be there for them. It's not about you.

**What you should do for someone in the midst of adversity:**

When in doubt regarding what you can say or do when you're talking to someone having a rough time, keep in mind these six basic guidelines:

- **Be positive.** You don't have to point out all the negatives they face, as they've likely already thought about them.

- **Be genuine.** Don't try to sound concerned if you're not, and don't make meaningless comments. No one has time for that; they will see right through it.

- **Remain in contact throughout their journey, recovery, and aftermath.** Don't be just a fair-weather friend because it makes you feel more comfortable.

- **Be sensitive in your actions and words.** Don't bring a deck of cards to someone who's just broken his arm, just as you wouldn't give a pack of cigarettes to someone battling lung cancer.

- **Don't make their ordeal about you.** Because it's not about you. What happened is happening to them.

- **Demonstrate that you care by your actions and not just your words.** What you do speaks volumes and will create a deeper connection.

**What you can say to someone in the midst of adversity:**

The good news is that some things are safe to say when someone is having a significant health issue or in the aftermath of a catastrophic event. Here are some to help you get started:

- **"This sucks!"** Why? It's true. Showing empathy is always better than sympathy.

- **"Your strength is impressive."** Why? Words of encouragement are essential.

- **"Did you watch last weekend's Saturday Night Live?"** Why? Talking about things other than sickness and adversity can be a welcome distraction. It can also help to normalize the moment for both of you.

- **"We can talk about whatever you'd like**, and if you need to vent your anger and complain, I'm here to listen." Why? Simply showing up and being there for your friend is powerful. Allowing them to talk about what they want to is an even greater gift.

- **"I will be coming to visit next week in the afternoon.** Would Tuesday or Wednesday work better for you?" Why? Asking if they would like you to visit can leave some people in a quandary because they don't want to bother or burden others. Don't ask if, but instead when. Then, bring them a fun treat they haven't asked for.

A long-time friend of mine was in a local hospital, dying in late December of 2022. His body was riddled with cancer that had metastasized. I drove over to spend some time with him during my lunch hour. He knew his time was short and that death was imminent. I pulled up a chair next to him, and for nearly an hour, we talked about his kids, the trip they had recently taken him on to Scottland, and the care his wife would need after he passed. He asked about my job and what it was like working for a company after over three decades of self-employment. He asked me to pray with him. I reached out and held his hand as we prayed. As I walked to the door when it was time for me to get back to work, Eric said, "Hey, Bob, Thank you for being real with me and not just saying a bunch of platitudes. I appreciate you." As Eric knew, things don't always get better. He passed two days later.

Recognizing the impact of words during difficult times reinforced how crucial it is to approach challenges with care and understanding. The lessons I learned became even more important as I faced the

ongoing, persistent waves of adversity that life continued to bring.

## Navigating Waves of Adversity

So how do we gain our footing before the next adversity tries to knock us on our collective asses? For me, I needed to find a balance between perspective, self-care, and healthy strategies. What helped me:

- **I prayed** for courage and the strength to make it through.

- **I looked for small wins,** including small goals that I could achieve daily.

- **I took moments to pause and breathe**—like, *actually breathe* with slow, deep breaths. Stress can cause us to either hyperventilate or freeze into a pattern of shallow breaths that prohibit carbon dioxide removal from our blood. (That's not good.)

- **I learned to be 'present,'** which means I didn't waste time thinking about the past or the stresses of tomorrow[31]. I learned to focus on today.

- **I established routines.** Daily routines helped provide stabilizing emotional anchors when life seemed to be unraveling. One example was my morning coffee (in my PEG tube), journaling, and exercise. If these routines are challenging to follow, make a plan and put it in your calendar.

- **I learned to adapt and work to accept** things that were out of my control.

- **I leaned on my 'tribe.'** Reaching out for help, encouragement, and pep talks from my inner circle was essential. I didn't have to face life's stresses alone.

- **I erased the word 'perfection' from my lexicon.** I placed my focus on growing stronger, not more perfect.

- **I was purposely kind to myself.** This is especially true for those who are self-critical. All we can do is do our best, which is enough.

---

[31] Matthew 6:34 New Living Translation (NLT)
"So don't worry about tomorrow, for tomorrow will bring its own worries. Today's trouble is enough for today.

- **I learned to reframe the narrative.** Those things that were 'bad' at first glance could usually be viewed for the upsides and positive features that can grow from them.

- **I learned to bend like grass in the wind.** Rigid grass breaks under the pressure of the wind. I worked on perfecting the art of bending when the winds of adversity came.

- Lastly, and potentially most importantly, I recommend **seeking professional counseling** for tools to help navigate the storms of adversity and for perspective and growth as adversities pass.

**Build a support system/network.**

Life's challenges are hard enough without having to face them alone, and isolating yourself and refusing help will only make things harder. In fact, accepting support from others is a sign of strength, not weakness. Research shows that strong social support can have a profound impact on our well-being, comparable in importance to avoiding harmful habits like smoking. A strong support network can be the difference between life and death.

Support networks—made up of friends, family, coworkers, or organized groups—help us navigate adversity by providing emotional, practical, and moral support. From assisting with everyday tasks after an accident to helping someone rebuild after a major loss, these networks ease the burden during tough times.

Support systems can vary in size and structure, with some being informal and spontaneous while others are carefully organized. They might include everything from temporary support from friends to formal programs like church groups or recovery organizations. Regardless of their structure, support networks are vital in helping people recover, rebuild, and move forward after hardships.

Recognizing the need for a support network is vital. Sometimes, it's obvious, like after losing a job or the family home burns down. Other times, friends and family may step in when we don't realize we need help —a support 'intervention' of sorts. Support quality matters more than quantity, regardless of whether the need is short-term or long-term. A dependable network ensures someone always has your back when life doesn't go as planned.

Support groups are available in most areas that focus on specific purposes, such as anger management, loss of a child, divorce, and others. Search online to find options in your city or county. Begin by searching:

- National Alliance on Mental Illness (NAMI[32])

---

[32] https://www.nami.org/Support-Education/Support-Groups

- Mental Health America (MHA[33])

- Anxiety and Depression Association of America (ADAA[34])

- Depression and Bipolar Support Alliance (DBSA[35])

- Substance Abuse and Mental Health Services Administration (SAMHSA[36])

- Cancer Support Community[37]

- Confident Health[38]

- 7 Cups[39]

- SupportGroups.com[40]

- Reddit Communities (search for *subreddits* such as r/GriefSupport[41] and r/Anger[42]

- Local community centers and hospitals

---

[33] https://mhanational.org/find-support-groups
[34] https://adaa.org/supportgroups
[35] https://tinyurl.com/2ubxj84p
[36] https://tinyurl.com/42kbhrhp
[37] https://www.cancersupportcommunity.org
[38] https://www.confidanthealth.com/virtual-support-groups
[39] https://www.7cups.com
[40] https://supportgroups.com
[41] https://www.reddit.com/r/GriefSupport/comments/1gjpxiq/support_group
[42] https://tinyurl.com/43n6hvdu

# A Life Rewritten

Everyone will face hardships over the course of a lifetime that test their limits, reshape their beliefs, and ultimately change who they are. My journey through compounded adversities has been a vivid example of the dual nature of struggle: it is both a relentless adversary and an unexpected mentor. My purpose in sharing my story is not to dwell on my calamities but to inspire, empower, and encourage others while helping them grow resilient and find purpose as they face life's challenges.

By the time you read this, I might already be gone. As of today, my father is 92 years old, and my mother is 91. My family has incredible longevity genes on both sides of the family tree. Unfortunately, even great genes cannot overcome the devastating effects of chemotherapy and excess radiation exposure on the body. I've learned I likely have less than a decade to live. I'm also at peace knowing my death will likely be slow rather than dropping dead from a heart attack. However, the damage to my cardiovascular system from chemotherapy makes my ultimate demise a tossup, I suppose. I realize this sounds morbid, but I wouldn't be able to write this without the peace in my heart that comes from knowing how blessed I am.

Being aware of an abbreviated future is a good thing. It brings into focus the time between now and when I pass. As the intro to the long-running soap opera says, "Like sands through the hourglass, so are the Days of our Lives." No matter how many days I've lived up till now, I am at peace knowing the days I have left are far fewer. In Lord of the Rings, Gandalf summed it up when he said, "All we have to decide is what to do with the time that is given to us."[43]

I am not a retiring politician with aspirations of having an airport named after me or a monument raised in my honor. I'm just a man who hopes his words of encouragement can inspire love, hope, courage, and forgiveness in those he encounters. If I can use the remainder of my days to give hope to strangers and demonstrate selflessness and unconditional love to my family and friends, I can die knowing I have been a good steward of my time to change the world around me for the better.

When adversity first entered my life, it wasn't with a warning alarm but a whisper—a stinging pain under my tongue that evolved into something far greater than I

---

[43] Tolkien, J. R. R. 1991. The Lord of the Rings. London, England: HarperCollins.

ever imagined. Over the years, cancer and I have gotten to know each other well. It took parts of my body, stripped away my voice, affected my ability to breathe, stole my ability to enjoy food, and repeatedly challenged my resilience. Yet, even as I lost the physical tool I relied upon to communicate, I found ways to more profoundly connect with others. Facing the uncertainty of each new surgery and adapting to life with an ever-changing body have taught me that true communication and true connection come from the heart. My voice might have changed, but my message remains clear: we are more than our circumstances, and our adversities don't define us.

One of the hardest lessons I've learned is that adversity rarely comes in manageable doses. It often arrives in waves—cancer, personal loss, business failures—testing not only my endurance but my spirit too. In those moments, it's easy to question why life seems so determined to break us and destroy us. I remember vividly the long nights alone, with tears that flowed freely, and the fear that this might be the chapter in which I would finally be defeated. But every setback carried within it an opportunity. Losing my ability to speak has helped me appreciate the power of silence and the importance of listening. It reminded me how often we take for granted the seemingly small blessings in life—like being able to share a simple conversation with the ones I love.

Sharing my journey has also provided opportunities for empathy. Seeing my daughters, family, and friends go through the pain of watching me suffer while trying to maintain a brave face was sometimes harder than enduring the treatments themselves. This hasn't been just my story; it has also been theirs. My daughter, Sara, was my fierce advocate and stood by my side in the hospital, holding my feet when my hands were covered with tubes and bandages. She stayed in the waiting room alone during my surgeries, not knowing if she'd see me smile again. My daughters, Ashley and Holly, gave their time to be at my side to see to my needs. Even in those moments of darkness, my family showed me that love is the greatest medicine—it nourishes, empowers, and sustains us.

Reflecting on my legacy led me to a haunting question: Would my younger self recognize who I have become and the life I have been blessed to live? No, but I am hopeful that my story—and what I've learned—will encourage those who read this book. Adversity is not just about what I've lost; it's about what I've gained in the process. I found purpose in being transparent about my journey. Recording my video blogs, writing these chapters, and speaking about my experiences (even when words were hard to form) became a means of turning my struggles into lessons to share with others. Cancer took my tongue, but it didn't take my ability to inspire. Each scar is a chapter in a larger story—one that, I hope, will help others find their own courage when they face the dark.

My faith has been my anchor throughout this journey. It has given me the strength to face each day with hope and the belief that there is a purpose in my pain. I know that God walks with me and that knowledge has provided comfort when nothing else could. It is my faith that allows me to see my situation not as a curse but as an opportunity to grow, to love, and to inspire others. When I think of the road ahead, I know I won't walk it alone. My faith gives me peace, knowing that even though my time here may be limited, I am part of a greater story that extends beyond this life's boundaries.

If there's one message I want readers to take away from my story, it's that adversity does not define us—our response to it does. We can't control the trials that life throws our way, but we can decide how we meet them. When faced with the unthinkable, we can choose to retreat into despair, or we can fight back with hope, resilience, and purpose. Nobody can take that choice from us. My life has been forever changed by the challenges I've faced, but it has also been made better by the lessons I've learned along the way. I want to be a beacon for others who feel overwhelmed, to remind them that they are never alone and that even if our voice falters, our spirit can still shout its message loud and clear: We are still here, we are still fighting, and we will not give up.

Reflecting on my rewritten life helped me realize my ultimate choice: Let hardship make me bitter or provide an opportunity for growth. This decision will ultimately shape the chapters that are yet to come.

# Epilogue

If I had my choice, I would want to die slowly. I've lost dear friends who died in an instant—one in a freak sporting event accident, another to a ritualistic murder, and others to suicide. I never got to say goodbye. So many friends have died instantly, leaving unfinished business behind. When they died, they left their friends, family, spouses, and children without a chance for closure. No chance to say "I'm sorry," to forgive and seek forgiveness, and no chance to offer encouraging words to those who needed an emotional hand up out of their pits of despair.

I've often said that "cancer is a blessing," which nearly always brings some to the point of rage, especially if they have watched a family member or friend go through it. The reason I say it is a blessing is because it allows the cancer patient to settle their affairs, make amends, and find closure before passing. It's part of why I've come to a place of peace about cancer attacking me. I know it could return at any time, so I must make the most of today because I might die tomorrow.

While I remain alive, I can choose to forgive someone who has wronged me or hold on to negative emotions that can halt my emotional growth. It is a choice. Forgiveness is not for the benefit of the person I am forgiving but for me because it releases me from the shackles of bitterness.

Every challenge I've faced has shaped who I am, leaving its mark—metaphorically and physically—and making me stronger. Each hardship taught me to stand tall, even when life felt overwhelming. Looking back, I see not just the struggles but also the victories—not just the pain but the growth.

This is the story of my life: shaped by challenges, strengthened by resilience, and guided by faith and hope. It's a journey of learning, finding light in dark times, and turning difficulties into stepping stones toward something greater.

I'm not a life coach or a self-enrichment motivational speaker, and I'm not one to put on a happy face while secretly feeling sad on the inside, but I am content and have a positive attitude because I choose to.

Some people scream at the sky, asking, 'Why me!?' I ask, 'Why not me?' knowing that I'm not more special than anyone else. I've put my faith in Jesus. That doesn't mean I need to be 'religious' or try to be perfect because I don't. What I do need to do is exactly what He said, which is to love God and love others[44]. The instructions I live by aren't any more complicated than that.

---

[44] Mark 12:30-31, Holy Bible

www.ingramcontent.com/pod-product-compliance
Lightning Source LLC
Chambersburg PA
CBHW071958040426
42447CB00009B/1381